D1483773

"In this erudite tome, Whitfield offers an account of martyrdom that refuses the shackles of liberal secular politics. Such refusal, however, is not rooted in a rejection of the world and its attempts to regulate sacred narratives; Whitfield reminds us that its refusal is predicated on the eschatological promise that God will bring all creation to completion. The witness of the martyr, is not a discourse about the individual agent; it is a discourse about the saving activity of the Triune God."

—**TRIPP YORK,** author of *The Purple Crown: The Politics of Martyrdom*

Pilgrim Holiness

To: Margarita,

Thanks for the
beauty of your
witness!

—Johnna

Pilgrim Holiness

Martyrdom as Descriptive Witness

JOSHUA J. WHITFIELD

Foreword by Stanley Hauerwas

CASCADE *Books* · Eugene, Oregon

PILGRIM HOLINESS
Martyrdom as Descriptive Witness

Cascade Books
An Imprint of Wipf and Stock Publishers
199 W. 8th Ave., Suite 3
Eugene, OR 97401

www.wipfandstock.com

ISBN 13: 978-1-60608-175-4

Cataloging-in-Publication data:

Whitfield, Joshua J.

　Pilgrim holiness : martyrdom as descriptive witness / Joshua J. Whitfield.

　xviii + 134 p. ; 20 cm. Includes bibliographical references.

　ISBN 13: 978-1-60608-175-4

　1. Martyrdom—Christianity. I. Title.

BR1601.3 .W45 2009

Manufactured in the U.S.A.

"*It is so little true that martyrs prove anything as to the truth of an affair, that I would fain deny that ever a martyr has had anything to do with truth.*"

—Friedrich Nietzsche, *The Antichrist*

Contents

Foreword

You can kill us, but you cannot determine the meaning of our deaths. No one can know who they are until God tells them who they are. Martyrs die confident that only God can determine the significance of their deaths. Indeed, martyrs do not die in order to be martyrs; martyrs cannot act intentionally toward their death. Rather they must avoid having to die. They must do so because they must desire to live, and they must desire to spare their murderers the burden of the murderers' sin.

We dare not, therefore, turn the martyrs into "heroes" or "heroines." They are martyrs. They are, as Joshua Whitfield argues in this haunting book, witnesses to the new time inaugurated by Jesus in which the violence of sin and death has been defeated. Heroism threatens to separate the martyr from the narrative and the community determined by that narrative which alone makes the martyr intelligible. Accordingly Whitfield helps us see that attempts by Christian and non-Christians to "police" the witness of the martyrs by making the martyrs the exemplification of a general category of heroic sacrifice must be challenged if we are rightly to know what we say when we say "martyr."

We are, therefore, in Whitfield's debt for challenging our attempts to explain martyrdom, particularly after September 11, 2001, in categories foreign to the way Christians should understand the world. Martyrdom is not, as many suggest the, "heroic endurance of hardship"; martyrdom is nothing other than dying with Christ. The Muslim martyr and the Christian martyr are not the same, but they are now joined by the common task to resist those who would interpret them as the exemplifications of *ressentiment* against modernity. And this is how a book on martyrdom turns out to be a book in political theory.

That should not be surprising if we remember that to be a martyr one must be remembered. Martyrdom requires a collective memory; it demands a people exist who may not themselves be called to martyrdom but who, like the martyrs, have also learned that they cannot determine the meaning of their deaths. Such a people are able to remember the martyrs because they believe that Christ has disarmed the powers—powers who draw on our fear of death—to sustain the hold they have over our lives. By remembering the martyrs the Church discovers it is possible to live nonviolently because the fear of death no longer has dominion over our lives. Christ has undone death.

Whitfield calls attention to Sanctus, one of the martyrs of the early church, who taunted by his torturers about why he would undergo such an ordeal could only reply, "I am a Christian." Those that tortured Sanctus tried to rob his death of all meaning. They would have him die a meaningless death made even more meaningless by using torture to make it doubtful that he was even a human being. Yet those who tortured and killed Sanctus could not defeat his witness because his witness participates in the very life of Christ. Sanctus's confession, "I am a Christian" is, therefore, all that can be as well as all that needs to be said.

Joshua Whitfield is first and foremost a priest. Anyone reading this book will discover he is a priest who is not only extremely erudite but is also a sophisticated theologian. But he is first and foremost a priest. Why is he, therefore, writing a book on martyrdom? Martyrdom seems a long way from the everyday demands placed on the work of an everyday priest. Neither Whitfield nor members of his church will face the challenge of martyrdom. But they will face the challenge of rightly remembering the martyrs. That task, a task Whitfield argues is at the heart of being a truthful witness to the world, turns out to be decisive for every task a priest performs.

I have never had any use for the distinction between theology proper and pastoral theology. Any theology that is not about the church and the ministry of the church is not theology. But if anyone is determined to distinguish pastoral theology from other theological disciplines, *Pilgrim Holiness* is the paradigm of how pastoral theology should be done. That is why I described this book as "haunting." It should haunt us because Joshua reminds us—a reminder we desperately need as people determined by a death-denying world—that our deaths and the deaths of the martyrs are inseparable. Moreover, our task of telling their stories is what enables us to live truthful lives.

Stanley Hauerwas
Duke Divinity School
October 2008

$\mathscr{P}$reface

THE LIGHT OF SINAI
AND THE LIGHT OF MARTYRDOM

In November of 2006 I was breathless and exhausted, struggling to climb the "Stairs of Repentance" that wind up *Jebel Musa* in Sinai. Most of those with whom I was traveling, my friends far more fit than I, had gone quickly up the mountain and out of sight. Warren Smith, our professor and guide, got stuck behind me on the narrow and sometimes treacherous mountain stairway. He is an experienced climber, so he became for me an indispensable support as I slowly struggled higher, each step more difficult than the last.

I had not realized how out of shape I was. Yet what soon became far more intense and burdensome that afternoon on the mountain was the unexpected spiritual trial that came to bear upon me with every new and more arduous step. Stopping as often as I did for water and rest, I was able to read the biblical account of Moses's ascent, of the danger and reality of the covenant given on Sinai. I was struck by how the promises of the kingdom and priesthood were so easily interspersed with apparently draconian warnings about not touching the mountain until the right moment, neither humans nor animals. I was more alert to the vivid accounts of enveloping smoke and flashing lightning that accompanied the theophany. Exhausted and reading the story of Israel's covenant, I became more sensitive than ever to the sometimes brutal physicality of Israel's encounter with God, to the danger and reality of Israel's need for God in the desert and on the mountain. It was possible for me to imagine just how the Israelites belonged then to a totally encompassing covenant that could only be lived out in the precarious, alert, and momentary existence of the desert. For Israel, the theophany on Sinai did not dissolve the daily particularity of life. It actually made life heavier, fuller, and thicker.

In my exhaustion I realized this on the mountain. Climbing, I was hunched over a lot, taking one and sometimes just two steps at a time. I rested my upper body on my knees as I heavily took one step after another. It was just after midday during our climb, and the sun was high in the cloudless sky. The light shined so brightly down on me hunched over and heavy that I could not see any higher than one or two steps. At first this was troubling in that I was completely unaware of whatever twists or turns awaited me, and I had no clue as to how much longer I had before reaching the top. Yet hunched over and with my heart pounding, I realized that all I needed to see at any one moment were the one or two steps in front of me. Frankly, it was unnecessary and even dangerous for me to wonder so much about the path ahead. The one or two steps I could see just before me were challenging and demanding enough. Had I been able to see too far ahead, I would not have given enough thought and care to the steps I had to take one at a time. The sun's light, blinding and limiting though it was, helped me to see what I needed to see when I needed to see it.

Speaking spiritually, this is the experience I discover again and again in the stories of the martyrs. To many the martyrs are blind ideologues who, sometimes through violence or terror, force their illusions upon the real world. Either through some bad version of eschatology or by some secret and coveted power, it is assumed that martyrs have traded the real for the delusional. Nietzsche growled that martyrs could never be trusted for truth, and perhaps this is the accepted wisdom among those of us content with present appearances.

This book hopes to argue against such accepted wisdom. It is my suggestion that martyrdom by no means trades upon a delusional transposition of bad religion or ideology with something called the "real" world. Rather, I contend that martyrdom, as an explicitly christological witness, offers limited but vital description within the various and unpredictable arenas of living, suffering, and death. That is, martyrdom is not the tragic conclusion of some fatal *idée fixe* but a momentary truthful glimpse of present circumstances. Martyrdom is something that reveals, clarifies, and illumines what we take for the real. It does not offer anyone an escape from the strictures of real life, suffering, and death. Instead, martyrdom offers descriptions more physical, more intense, and more lasting. Stephen saw heaven thrown open just as much as he saw the stones flying toward his head.

Stephen also saw enough to forgive his murderers. And this is why martyrdom is still important for the church today. The martyrs exemplify truthful living—humble, peaceful, limited, and burdened living within a world that has yet to acknowledge the Lord. So easily religion and religious people can be tricked into the service of lesser, more sinister myths. The martyrs are significant for the church today because they exhibit that sort of truthful living which refuses the claims of history and power without Christ and which show the sort of living and dying that returns forgiveness upon murder and patience beyond domination. In this sense the martyrs are anti-ideologues in that they choose suffering and peaceable patience over the systems of governments, philosophers, or theologians. The martyrs are blinded enough by the light of Christ to see the truth of the present moment; and so, as in so many accounts, the martyrs leave behind them forgiveness and peace, the discovered gifts of truthfulness. This is what happened in Lyons:

> Nor did they gloat over those who had fallen; rather, they gave of their own abundance to those in need, showing to them a maternal love, shedding many tears on their behalf before the Father. Life was what they asked for and he gave it to them, and this they shared with their neighbour when they went off completely victorious to God. Peace they had always loved, and it was peace which they commended to us for ever. In peace they departed to God, leaving no pain for their Mother, no strife or conflict for their brothers, but rather joy, peace, harmony, and love.[1]

Such are the fruits of truthfulness in the martyrs' description of the world. It is perhaps the best Christians can or should do. This book explores such descriptive and peaceful witness, hoping that we can learn to hope as the martyrs once did—suffering for truth instead of killing for its false idol.

Deo gratias agimus: Stanley Hauerwas, Warren Smith, J. R. and Hannah Rigby, Alex Sider, Charles Bellinger, Natalie Carnes, Lukas Von Rompey, Reinhard Hütter, Timothy Kimbrough, Jo Bailey and Samuel Wells, Douglas Campbell, Miguel Romero, Hugh Houghton, Melissa Meredith, the Church of Saint Peter and Saint Paul, Arlington, Texas, the Church of the Holy Family, Chapel Hill, North Carolina, the Church of Saint Gregory the Great, Mansfield, Texas, my family and for Alli.

Joshua J. Whitfield
The Annunciation 2008

---

1. *The Martyrs of Lyons* 2.6–7.

CHAPTER I

𝔓olicing the 𝔐artyrs
A YODERIAN DEMONOLOGY

"But to those miserable men, witness to the Lord
by blood seems a most violent death . . ."

—Clement of Alexandria *Stromata* 4.7

PROFITABLY POLICING THE MARTYRS

𝔖ince at least the time of Celsus at the end of the second century, there has always been literature virulently critical of the church. What is remarkable, however, is that although the church has indeed responded with its own massive volumes of polemics and apologies, the best of these defensive works admit, in some sense, their own futility. Origen, for example, at the beginning of his own long work against Celsus, shows his reluctance to answer these attacks by pointing to Jesus, silent in the face of his own accusers. Despite Origen's own efforts, he suggests that "even now he [Jesus] continues silent before these things, and makes no audible answer, but places his defense in the lives of his genuine disciples, which are a pre-eminent testimony."[1]

---

1. Origen *Against Celsus* 1.2.

It is rather, Origen insists—however conceitedly—the life of the church itself that provides the best response to criticism and attack. Today the tradition of Celsus and others continues strong but in a thoroughly fictional key. Now, books and other media critical of religion constitute an industry that is currently in rather profitable bloom. In turn, an industry of religious apologetics has emerged, with each publishing house organizing digestible polemical bouts for the sake of the buying public. They are these competing currents, together making eddies in the flow of marketed ideas, which trap those interested in these controversies and who are willing to pay for and profit from a fray marketable enough for the masses. Of course, now it is all fiction. Once hunting was for survival, today it is a sport.

The vast and diverse popular literature that funds so much of what passes for conventional thought and conversation is about something called "religion." It is something called "religion" more than it is religion itself, for in the very parsing out of their polemical targets, contemporary authors succeed in destroying something that is completely fictional. That is, put simply, what they build up to tear down is nothing other than what they have themselves constructed. Yet what these authors do indeed show by their religious parodies is the largely fictional status of religion for many of those who believe. For we should recognize that, far too often, people of faith as well as people not of faith accept the terms of current debates about "religion"—terms that presuppose the absence of the Church. Thus that which constituted "Christian faith" for Origen—namely, the doctrine of Christ bodied forth in the "lives of genuine disciples"—has been abandoned by believers and unbelievers alike. This is to suggest that the current industry of media either for or against "religion" is itself a reflection upon and indeed the result of the present diminishment and humiliation of the church. It is in perceived ecclesial absence where these battles are fought. The church is certainly mentioned in these books, foisted back and forth as either a villainous, powerful, and ignorant institution or as the unfaltering ark of truth and salvation, albeit largely mystically invisible or magisterially impregnable. In both instances, the church exists only as a static fiction.

Such is the fictional status of this industry. I do not mean to say that these profitable quarrels do no real service at all. Quite the opposite: they serve to police sacred narratives in service of secular ones. In providing a marketed and fictional space for the interrogation of "religion," the anxiety of an imagined secular modernity is relieved insofar as sacred narratives are treated in what is commercially quarantined as entertainment and leisure. This is the first and great policing of sacred narratives in which the industry of polemics is located. It is but one feature of the liquid individuality of churchless modernity.[2]

There is yet another policing of sacred narratives, and this is found within anti-religious literature itself. Each book presently popular takes different angles and adds its own unique diagnosis. Some are more serious and certainly more scientific, as in the case of Richards Dawkins's *The God Delusion* or Daniel Dennett's *Breaking the Spell*. Others are far less serious, such as Sam Harris's *The End of Faith* and Christopher Hitchens's *God is Not Great*. Some, like Dennett, primarily criticize Christianity. Others, like Harris, attack Islam on behalf of other religions. All of these, however, make similar arguments for the inadmissibility of the claims of any one particular religion. The arguments are simple: religion is defined as a phenomenon, thereby removing the necessity to deal seriously with the particularity of any religion in question. As a phenomenon, religion is then associated with an intellectual and moral absolutism that is deemed historically culpable of all or most of the previous violence of

2. See Bauman, *Liquid Modernity*, ch. 2.

history as well being judged presently politically dangerous. This conviction of religion is often expressed in terms of an evolutionary development away from the irrational, showing secular politics to be the proper end of the troubled and halted progress of humanity.

Dennett, for example, must first define what he intends to break. Religion must be basically definable as the various phenomena of "social systems whose participants avow belief in a supernatural agent or agents whose approval is to be sought."[3] And it is just this that is the problem, for, according to Dennett, religion destroys any democratic possibility. Dennett's "sacred values" are "democracy, justice, life, love, and truth;"[4] however, should there be any claims made about the specific or ultimate character of those values without meeting empirical criteria, those claims become obstacles in the way of realizing what Dennett can only fetishistically call "values," a nominal change betraying the vacuity of what used to name virtues, transcendentals, or modes of politics, or discipleship. Religion, to put it simply, is antithetical to democracy, for the religious claim to be able to narrate Dennett's sacred values allegedly ends the democratic process before it begins.[5] This fear betrays a misunderstanding of both religion and democracy. Nevertheless, for Dennett and others, religion thus defined, fosters a politically very dangerous absolutism.[6] For Harris, this makes for an explicit connection between religion and violence. Belief dictates action; absolute belief dictates absolute action.[7] This is simply violence in the political sphere. Thus, for Harris,

3. Dennett, *Breaking the Spell*, 9.

4. Ibid., 23.

5. Ibid., 14.

6. Ibid., 285.

7. Harris, *End of Faith*, 12.

religion is the "explicit" cause of "millions of deaths."[8] Faith, for Harris, is the "mother of hatred"[9]; and likewise, for Dawkins, it "is an evil precisely because it requires no justification and brooks no argument."[10] This is simply the seed of absolutism, and, for Dawkins, "it constitutes a major reason for suggesting that religion can be a force for evil in the world."[11]

The deadly apogee of faith in these arguments is what Harris calls the "metaphysics of martyrdom."[12] According to Hitchens, the absolutism of religion must tend toward interference, violence, domination, and martyrdom: "It *must* seek to interfere with the lives of nonbelievers, or heretics, or adherents of other faiths. It may speak about the bliss of the next world, but it wants power in this one."[13] Religion as absolutism makes for martyrdom in that it provokes a psychological crisis, the political consequence of which is religious violence. "What," Dennett asks, "are all those young men going to do with themselves? We have a few years to figure out benign channels into which their hormone-soaked energies can be directed."[14] For Dennett and others, martyrdom names a psychological crisis of identity, which is dressed in terms of moral development and evolution. Martyrdom is the representative event of psychological, moral, and political archaism.

Such is how martyrdom is first policed within anti-religious literature: by rendering it a pre-secular artifact. This policing is completed in the banishment of sacred narratives (and thus, it is assumed, violence) from politics. Here Dennett is explicit:

8. Ibid., 26.

9. Ibid., 30.

10. Dawkins, *God Delusion*, 308.

11. Ibid., 286.

12. Harris, *End of Faith*, 14.

13. Hitchens, *God is Not Great*, 17.

14. Dennett, *Breaking the Spell*, 333.

> If you decline to put your beliefs on the line, then your beliefs, whatever they are, really cannot be given any consideration in the ongoing investigation, which has no use for one-sided declarations that will not be subjected to rigorous scrutiny and cross-examination.[15]

Harris, whose first target is Islam (he says explicitly, "We are at war with Islam"[16]), puts this in even starker terms. Religion, as for the others, names an archaic reliquary of unsupportable beliefs,[17] any benefits of which could be assumed by a "mature science of the mind,"[18] described as rational mysticism[19] free of any particular dogma.[20] Secular ethics and politics based upon reason and purely evidentiary claims show the West's advanced moral development and wealth.[21] This is what Harris calls "civil society," a political space free of the absolutism of sacred narratives and the havoc they cause, "where ideas, of all kinds, can be criticized without the risk of physical violence."[22] Politics without violence: this is the illusory good and deep irony of the political secularism and rationalism advocated by Harris and others. It is, it turns out, not a matter of avoiding violence, but of selecting violence and preferring one form of violence over others. Harris is frank in his proposals. "It appears," he says, "that one of the most urgent tasks we now face in the developed world is to find some way of facilitating the emergence of civil societies everywhere else."[23] But of course, given the lack

15. Ibid., 359.

16. Harris, *End of Faith*, 109.

17. Ibid., 23.

18. Ibid., 20.

19. Ibid., 221.

20. Ibid., 41.

21. Ibid., 143.

22. Ibid., 150.

23. Ibid.

of moral development among Muslim countries, democracy is too risky and virtually unattainable.[24] What these countries need, Harris suggests, is a "benign dictatorship," preferably under the administration of a world government.[25] This must be achieved, argues Harris, as a matter of survival. Thus violence, here in the service of civil society, is appropriate and necessary. "Given the power of our technology," Harris claims, "we can see at a glance that aspiring martyrs will not make good neighbors."[26] Fearing nuclear annihilation at the hands of an "Islamist regime," Harris hopes "that the forces of secularism and rationality will keep the missiles in their silos for a while yet,"[27] not just for defense against a religious nuclear attack but for possible offensive violence:

> In such a situation, the only thing likely to ensure our survival may be a nuclear first strike of our own. Needless to say, this would be an unthinkable crime— as it would kill tens of millions of innocent civilians in a single day—but it may be the only course of action available to us, given what Islamists believe.[28]

Civil society, a space allegedly free of violence, is secured, albeit violently. However, the violence of civil society is considered morally different as it is based upon the rational principles of evidentiary science.[29] The practitioners of Western violence have the capacity for shock and remorse when their appropriate intentions for violence are exceeded, unlike the religious celebrants of martyrdom and holy war who pursue potentially limitless

24. Ibid., 132.
25. Ibid., 151.
26. Ibid., 48.
27. Ibid., 28.
28. Ibid., 129.
29. Ibid., 146.

destruction.[30] For Harris, violence waged for secularism is of a different metaphysical and moral order. Secular rationality, so it seems, redeems all violence.

There are a few issues here to address. As will be seen below with others, what Harris illustrates is that the crime of the martyrs, or of religious killers, is not that they have killed or have rashly allowed themselves to be killed. Rather, the particular offense of religious violence is seeking out religious and political identity incongruent with the terms of liberal secular politics. This is the contradiction and irony at the center of Harris's and others' policing of sacred narratives. As Talal Asad suggests, there is in the "liberal West's culture of war" the political necessity "to legitimize organized violence against a collective enemy (including civilians)" as well as the "humanitarian desire to save lives."[31] However, such humanitarianism is highly selective. It seeks "not the protection of life as such but the construction and encouragement of specific kinds of human subjects and the outlawing of all others."[32] For Asad, this is what policing martyrdom as a religious phenomenon serves. It is a model that provides psychological and cultural differentiation that "lends itself to the discourse of the protection of civilization (committed to life) against barbarism (a love of death)."[33] This is correct but only partially. As will be argued below, although Asad sufficiently complicates the "simple agenitive model"[34] of Harris and others, he does not address the martyrs' or religious killers' claims themselves. Asad realizes this further need that "if one is to talk about religious subjectivities, one must work through

30. Ibid., 144.

31. Asad, *On Suicide Bombing*, 16.

32. Ibid., 36.

33. Ibid., 56.

34. Ibid., 15.

the concepts the people concerned actually use."[35] This, however, is an investigation below the rationality of Harris and others; nonetheless, this is precisely the discourse that must be allowed—sacred narratives must be admitted as sacred although contingent. That is, the words and deeds of martyrs or religious killers must be read by light of the particular narratives they claim to embody. Such reading must be done if there is to be any genuine understanding of those accepting death or of those who kill for what they believe. Yet this is precisely what is not allowed in contemporary anti-religious literature, and so the policing of martyrdom in these works is complete.

Again, it must be underscored that this is fictional discourse in an industry of fiction. This literature constructs and defeats its own fabricated enemies. The anti-religious accuser in this literature is also a staged player in the theater of the leisured anxiety of modernity. As they police their parodies of religion and martyrdom, so too are they policed by the fluctuating attention of the market. This is the double policing effect of the media—everything, story and story-teller, is rendered holographic on the television or on the computer screen. So it is made a commodity.

This is only one way, however, by which the martyrs are policed. Taking Asad's suggestion that "one must work through the concepts the people concerned actually use," another double policing will be described below. Looking at the martyr traditions of Islam, Christianity, and Judaism, and then at how they are described and explained, parallel arguments will emerge. One argument for policing, internal to the particular religion in question and thus legitimate, will emerge beside an argument mostly external to any particular religion. This latter argument

35. Ibid., 44. In the epilogue (95) Asad addresses the need for further genealogical research in this area. This, it seems to me, is an invitation for theology—Muslim, Christian, and so forth.

is, in some sense, illegitimate, repeating and funding the explanations that have already been encountered above. Only after this has been shown, can there be any room for listening to the martyrs themselves.

POLICING THE MARTYRS OF ISLAM

Martyrdom within Islam has its own complex and fluid history. From the Qur'an up to the present day, that which has constituted martyrdom within Islam has involved not only conflict over the very nature of Islam among Muslims themselves, it has also involved a complicated rhetorical engagement with non-Muslims trying to grasp the sometimes differing theological and political claims of various advocates of Islam. The struggle to describe martyrdom and *jihad* within Islam in many ways names an identity crisis among Muslims; however, it also names a crisis in the largely non-Muslim West, both crises being in some sense congenital. This was true in the seventh century, and it is true today as debates over martyrdom have reemerged in the numerous revived *jihad* movements of the latter half of the twentieth century up to the present day. Over the centuries, martyrdom in Islam has been subject to a double policing: first, and more legitimately by Muslims themselves, namely by the *'ulama*, and second, roughly speaking, by those in the West.

From the very beginning of the Prophet's career, struggle for the complete realization of Islam was consequent in the very genesis of Muhammad's message. From the circumstances forcing the Prophet's first *hijra* to Medina through the Islamic political expansion of the following centuries, the theological claim was clear: "Your God is the one God: there is no god except Him, the Lord of Mercy, the Giver of Mercy."[36] Early on for the culturally and economically vulnerable in Mecca, following

36. *Sura* 2:163.

the Prophet invited remarkable suffering, as in the case of Bilal the Ethiopian who was forced to lay on the sunburnt ground with a heavy stone on his chest, or the female servant Sumayya who was beaten and then eventually stabbed to death for being associated with Muhammad.[37] After the Prophet's theocratic establishment in Medina, however, those proclaiming the message of Muhammad took on an active struggle to bring about the political recognition of revelation in the form of an Islamic *Umma* that would eventually become an empire.[38]

In the construction of Islam in its earliest centuries, martyrdom underwent a connotative evolution, the genealogy of which reveals early Islamic negotiations with not only neighboring Christian traditions of martyrdom, but also among Muslims, themselves, concerned with the political concord of the new Islamic *Umma*. The Arabic word *shahada* is found in the Qur'an in several passages but never in the nominative sense of the early Christian martyrs. *Shahada* in the Qur'an always refers to the act of witnessing, either of God to humanity,[39] or to humanity on behalf of God, or to the Prophet on behalf of God or humanity,[40] each witness being in some sense a *shahid*, confessing the truth of Allah in any given situation. Death, however, is not constitutive of *shahada* in the Qur'an as it is for Christian martyrdom; rather, it simply names the event of confession. Arguably lending to its later connotation with death, however, is that *shahada* is a cognate of the Syriac word *sāhdā*, primarily a word in Christian use in the seventh century.[41] It was the Christian martyr tradition that would partially account for this connotative shift in later

37. Cook, *Martyrdom in Islam*, 14.

38. Lewis, *Middle East*, 53.

39. *Sura* 6:18.

40. *Sura* 22:78.

41. Goldziher, *Muslim Studies*, 351. See also Cook, *Martyrdom in Islam*, 16.

Islamic thinking about *shahada*.[42] But perhaps what answers more for the specific connection between *shahada* and death is the specifically Qur'anic notion of *jihad*. In the eighth and ninth *suras*, commenting on the Battle of Badr in 624, the Prophet made clear that "it was God's will to establish the truth according to His Word and to finish off the disbelievers—to prove the Truth to be true, and the false to be false, much as the guilty dislike it."[43] Not only were angels at war alongside the Prophet's followers who were obligated to fight, it was God in battle who was ultimately responsible for victory:

> It was not you who killed them but God, and when you [Prophet] threw sand at them it was not your throw [that defeated them] but God's, to do the believers a favour: God is all seeing and all knowing— "That is what you get!"—and God will weaken the disbelievers' designs.[44]

Likewise, God was in possession of the faithful, having "purchased the persons and possessions of the believers in return for the Garden—they fight in God's way: they kill and are killed."[45] Yet it was not until the Battle of Uhud in 625 when the Prophet's army suffered significant losses that the heroic aura of fighting in the way of Allah took on any cultic imagination. Wondering about the fate of those fallen in battle, the Prophet relates to the survivors, "do not think of those who have been killed in God's way as dead. They are alive with their Lord, well provided for, happy with what God has given them of His favour."[46] These

---

42. Lewinstein, "Revaluation of Martyrdom," 79.

43. *Sura* 8:7–8.

44. *Sura* 8:17–18.

45. *Sura* 9:111. See also *Sura* 2:207: "But there is also a kind of man who gives his life away to please God, and God is most compassionate to His servants."

46. *Sura* 3:169.

were the theological and political factors at play in the earliest days of the Prophet, supplying a rather particular concept of *shahid* as one committed to *jihad*. It would be an inappropriate misreading to conclude that the figure of one committed to *jihad* outlined in the Qur'an is aggressive. Rather, the inauguration of *jihad* is understood to be defensive[47] and limited,[48] and coercion is renounced.[49] *Jihad* was in essence, and thus very ambiguously, understood as the struggle to "lift the Word of Allah to the highest."[50] Nonetheless, from the beginning, martyrdom in Islam was in constant negotiation as it is even today.

It is in the *hadith* material where the now uniquely Islamic but volatile doctrine of martyrdom developed further. Here are all the elaborate rewards to be found: nine, traditionally, including the immediate forgiveness of sins and admission into paradise, marriage to the *houris*, the Crown of Dignity, the ability to intercede for relatives and so on.[51] However, in the *hadith* literature there is a broadening of "the definition of martyrdom to the point where it began to lose all meaning and simply came to cover anyone who had died a worthy death and should be admitted immediately into paradise."[52] Occasions for martyrdom came to number no less than seven, anything from dying of stomach problems, drowning, or from a building collapse to being eaten by wild animals or dying from lovesickness. Cook argues that this broadening definition of martyrdom reflects the political establishment and settlement of an Islamic empire, when dying from disease or accident was more likely than dying

47. *Sura* 22:39.
48. *Sura* 2:190.
49. *Sura* 2:256.
50. Cook, *Martyrdom in Islam*, 30.
51. Lewinstein, "Revaluation," 81.
52. Cook, *Martyrdom in Islam*, 33.

at the hands of non-Muslims.[53] For Lewinstein, however, the *hadith* material reveals a negotiation within Islam itself more than mere political settlement. The Khārijites represented an aggressive element in early Islam. Responsible for the murder of 'Alī in 661,[54] the Khārijite ideal of martyrdom was that it was something deliberately sought, following the Qur'anic verse, "Let those of you who are willing to trade the life of this world for the life to come, fight in God's way."[55] In the broadening definition of martyrdom in the *hadith* literature, Lewinstein argues, is reflected the conflict and eventual triumph of scholars over the more militant interpretations of the Qur'an.[56]

Roughly speaking, these rival versions of martyrdom played out as Islam grew and diversified. Martyrdom in the more violent sense thrived among the Shi'ites, a minority sect in Islam and traditional plaintiffs for the rights of the familial descendents of the Prophet. Symbolic of their very identity and theology of martyrdom is the murder of al-Husayn at Karbala, Iraq, in 680. His death at the hands of an Umayyad governor would constitutively mark Shi'ism, according to Cook, with a profound sense of the transcendent utility of grief, expiation, and death as the very basic elements of Shi'ism.[57] This would fuel the readiness for death in later Shi'ite generations, evident even in the twentieth century among the Bassidj martyrs of Iran and Hezbollah in Lebanon.

Another version of martyrdom developed in Sufism beginning in the eighth century. The first Sufi ascetics, albeit fascinated with mystical union with God, were still prone to

53. Ibid., 35.

54. Lewis, *Middle East*, 66.

55. *Sura* 4:74.

56. Lewinstein, "Revaluation of Martyrdom," 86.

57. Cook, *Martyrdom in Islam*, 59.

fighting their Byzantine and Turkish enemies.[58] However, in the following centuries under the influence of such thinkers as al-Ghazali and al-Rumi, Sufi understanding of martyrdom took on a more purely ascetic and mystical hue. There emerged within Sufi thought a distinction between greater and lesser *jihad*, the latter naming an outward militant struggle and the former an inward and spiritual contest.[59] This, according to Cook, opened up Islam, ripening a more spiritual and thus more acceptable message that was able to be more widely embraced beyond the Arab and Persian world. Indeed, it was this version of Islam that was responsible for most of the large-scale conversions to Islam throughout the world.[60]

These intra-Islamic negotiations as to what constitutes martyrdom have continued to this day. Cook argues that over the last century there has been a revived interest and discussion about martyrdom within Islam correlative to the growing discontent with colonialism and the secular pan-Arabic nationalism evident in the Middle East since at least Atatürk. In Egypt, Iran, and Pakistan beginning in the 1950s there emerged what would be described as a "radical" revival of jihadism among Muslims distrustful of what was understood to be apostate secular governments. Since 1948, anti-Semitism came to mark these movements, fueling suspicions that the West, in establishing and supporting Israel, was conspiring to obliterate Islam.[61] This revival of *jihad* has not only involved Shi'ites but Sunnis as well, as the perception of the threat to Islam has grown.[62]

---

58. Ibid., 64.
59. Ibid., 73.
60. Ibid., 74.
61. Ibid., 137.
62. Brown, "Martyrdom in Sunni Revivalist Thought," 107.

Since the rise of so-called "martyrdom operations," or suicide attacks, the controversy over just what makes for martyrdom in Islam has intensified. The two traditionally rival versions of martyrdom have reemerged mostly along ideologically East/West lines. Among the more militant advocates of martyrdom, support for martyrdom operations has grown. Originally seen as a method intended only against Israel, martyrdom operations have been more and more accepted among certain *'ulama* in the Middle East.[63] This, of course, is in stark contrast to arguments of a particularly Sufi heritage, reemphasizing the greater inner *jihad* over a more militant struggle.[64]

All of the above, albeit described very briefly, represent an argument that is basically internal to Islam itself. However, this argument has not been closed off and isolated from the non-Muslim world. Sufism, in particular, reflects an ability basic to Islam to adapt, assimilate, and absorb the non-Muslim world. However, it is an argument that has roughly developed within the assumptions of Islam. Even despite sectarian division, the priority of the Qur'anic vision has remained intact. Alongside this internal argument, constituting a legitimate policing of Islamic martyrs, there is a predominantly Western policing of the martyrs of Islam. The character of this latter, and in some sense illegitimate, policing of these martyrs is that they seek to locate what they describe as the "phenomenon" of martyrdom within some other more determinative mold than in that which is constitutive of the martyrs themselves. This policing relies either on a "history of religions" approach to martyrdom, or on more purely sociological or psychological structures in order to neutralize the claims of the martyrs themselves. Just as with the popular policing of the martyrs, in what appears to be the harm-

63. Cook, "Implications of 'Martyrdom Operations,'" 131.

64. Cook, *Martyrdom in Islam*, 147.

less non-theological parsing of martyrdom as a phenomenon, lay the secret desire for the elimination of the sacred itself.

In the influential 1921 monograph *The Oriental Doctrine of the Martyrs*, A. J. Wensinck argued that Islam and Christianity, "as cognate phenomena," are to be understood essentially as "exponents of Hellenistic monotheism."[65] Building on the Syriac-Arabic connection of *shahada* and *sāhdā*,[66] Wensinck pushes the philological argument further back into the Maccabean writings, reading 4 Maccabees as essentially a Greek production:

> The whole passage in IV Maccabees is essentially Hellenistic in its ideas as well as in the picture of the scene and in the terminology. The "martyr" is really a philosopher, who is opposed to his counterpart the "tyrant." The latter is lord of outward things; the whole scene however is dominated by the other, who commands a spiritual authority which is much more important; the tyrant compels, the philosopher is really free.[67]

This is also basically a Stoic production that, according to Wensinck, was readily adopted in late Judaism, Christianity, and Islam.[68] The essential definition of martyrdom, therefore, holds throughout: it is the heroic endurance of hardship.[69] In Islam the widening definition of martyrdom reflects not negotiations within Islam but instead the re-assimilation of pre-Islamic folk wisdom.[70] Wensinck's historical and philological work, excellent in itself, cannot help but serve to reduce and eventually eliminate the possibility of a theology (and ultimately the sacrality) of

65. Wensinck, *Oriental Doctrine of the Martyrs*, 174.

66. Ibid., 155.

67. Ibid., 161.

68. Ibid., 162.

69. Ibid., 166.

70. Ibid., 172.

martyrdom in either Islam, Judaism, or Christianity, subordinating these particular accounts of martyrdom to the hegemony of an ambiguously defined Hellenism and to the mists of pre-Islamic custom.

This method of subordination is present in contemporary Western writing on martyrdom. David Cook's *Martyrdom in Islam*, a very fine scholarly work, nonetheless accepts from the very start an essential definition of martyrdom "that is identifiable and fairly constant through different faiths."[71] His definition is sociological. Following Eugene and Anita Weiner's analysis, Cook accepts their threefold definition of martyrdom, involving namely confrontation, motive, and narrative.[72] These elements, which are basically the dominant features of numerous martyrs' stories, serve here to define martyrdom itself. These features of their accounts, according to Weiner, both produce and perpetuate the martyr's "conviction," that is, the ineffable meaning of the martyr's life. Yet, the notion of conviction, as it is used by Weiner throughout the book, is irredeemably irrational.[73] Conviction is only and can only be an irrational device of an individual or group that must remain in constant tension with an equally ambiguous idea of the therapeutic sensitivity of the individual. This, according to Weiner, is the drama of all ethics.[74] It is not surprising, given the perceived ineluctable tension between irrational social conviction and the fragile therapeutic rationality of the individual, that Weiner's sociological analysis recommends an anxious attitude of "skepticism, admiration and fear,"[75] contemplating its own false dilemma of the necessity of irrational conviction and welfare of the rational

71. Cook, *Martyrdom in Islam*, 1.

72. Weiner and Weiner, *Martyr's Conviction*, 11–13.

73. Ibid., 1.

74. Ibid., 136.

75. Ibid., 138.

self. What was once perhaps a legitimate fear of the Prophet's message or a Christian's confession has become in sociological analysis a fear of the sacred itself.

In his analysis of revivalist *jihad*, especially those that have used suicide attacks, Farhad Khosrokhavar locates these movements well within modernity:

> Throughout the twentieth century, the modern world strove to relegate religion to the realm of the private affairs of the individual. Over the last decades, however, we have seen the return in force of ostentatious forms of religiosity that defy the public space they invest. They reject society, and may even declare war on it.[76]

For Khosrokhavar, contemporary militant jihadism does not issue from any pre-modern enclaves or sub-cultures of the Middle East; rather, "such terrorists are, in a way, products of our world."[77] The suicide attacks, characteristic of militant forms of *jihad* are, in his opinion, representatives of something entirely new, something that is only faintly Islamic.[78] For him, contemporary martyrdom names primarily a frustrated assertion of individuality, "an extreme situation characterized by the difficult advent of a process of individuation and by the failure of secular forms of modernization, which have the expectations of autonomy without actually satisfying them."[79] This is a crisis that is particularly acute among the marginalized youth in destabilized Muslim communities.[80] For Khosrokhavar, the psychological progress to martyrdom, although in a thin dress of Islamic mythology, is essentially Nietzschean. What answers

76. Khosrokhavar, *Suicide Bombers*, 1.

77. Ibid., 3.

78. Ibid., 37.

79. Ibid., 45.

80. Ibid., 54.

for the making of contemporary, quasi-Islamic martyrs is *ressentiment*, identity and values manufactured and governed by the irrational hatred of the other. Martyrdom in this case is explicitly a pathology of modernity—"martyropathy." [81]

There are two problems with Khosrokhavar's explanation of martyrdom here that are to the point. First, although he is correct to suggest that contemporary jihadist martyrdom is ineluctably a product of modernity, in never questioning the construction of modernity itself and, indeed, in even demanding the basically Kantian relegation of the sacred and theological to the ineffable, sublime, and irrational,[82] Khosrokhavar discounts the possibility of sacred narratives and politics peacefully occupying the same space. For Khosrokhavar, Islam has been corrupted to the extent that it has been secularized and made political.[83] Al-Husayn, symbolic martyr central to Shi'ism, has, according to him, been corrupted by being humanized and rendered imitable,[84] a dangerous mythological proxy for theocratic regimes such as Khomeini's Iran[85] or for the suicide bombers of Hamas. The problem here is not his suspicion of religious people and their motivation; rather, it is his apparently noncritical acceptance of the power of allegedly secular politics. *Ressentiment*, for Nietzsche, radically polarizes slave and master, completely externalizing the power of the master over the slave[86] who in turn subversively suffers the master only with the comforts of apocalyptic judgment.[87] Yet despite slave dreams

81. Ibid., 59.

82. Ibid., 58.

83. Ibid., 27.

84. Ibid., 40.

85. Ibid., 101.

86. Nietzsche, *Genealogy of Morals*, 1.10.

87. Ibid., 1.15.

of a kingdom come, fundamental to Nietzsche's notion of *ressentiment* is the unquestioned association of legitimate power with an ambiguously defined master. "To demand of strength that it should *not* express itself," is for Nietzsche absurd.[88] In Khosrokhavar's case, however, the power of the master is not as ambiguous as it was for Nietzsche; rather, it is unquestionably associated with the modern nation-state, a modern master that impresses back onto the slave body its own identity:

> In societies that have long been united under the aegis of a nation-state, we often forget that a country is almost an extension of the body and that, as he moves around his country, the individual has a feeling of being at home that is experienced inside the body. We are at one with our bodies in the same way that we experience our identity as something permanent, despite our changing moods and states of mind. A real country means an autonomous administration, a state of one's own, an autonomous mode of organization that is a reminder of a national identity, or in other words a body of phenomena constructed with reference to a homogeneous geography that is reminiscent of the unity of our own bodies.[89]

The crime of suicide bombers, therefore, is not that they have killed. Rather, it is that they have sought an identity and the necessarily consequent prerogatives of legitimate violence outside of the state. Thus, Asad's suggestion is basically correct that "typical explanations of the suicide bomber," such as Khosrokhavar's, "tell us more about the liberal assumptions of religious subjectivities and political violence than they do about what is ostensibly being explained."[90] For Khosrokhavar, the assumptions are

88. Ibid., 1.13.

89. Khosrokhavar, *Suicide Bombers*, 135.

90. Asad, *On Suicide Bombing*, 42.

metaphysically Kantian and politically Nietzschean, although in a way that Nietzsche himself would probably despise. For by implicating the state in the formation of identity, and in turn by narrating martyrdom as an identity crisis, Khosrokhavar affords the state a psychological authority Nietzsche would have rejected. Moreover, in associating state and identity, the violence employed by the state takes on the aura of psychological correction. Asad's point applies here: in narrating contemporary martyrdom as an identity crisis in quasi-Islamic dress, the suicide attacker can sufficiently be defined as "morally underdeveloped" in comparison "with peoples whose civilized status is partly indicated by their secular politics and their private religion and whose violence is therefore in principle disciplined, reasonable, and just."[91]

Khosrokhavar displays the complete policing of the martyrs of Islam. As with the other examples of the illegitimate policing of Islamic martyrs, sacred narratives are always identified with the irrational and are therefore always inappropriately present in political space. The issue is not the justice or injustice of killing, being killed or murder; rather, the issue concerns just who may kill and be killed and who may murder and for what reasons—questions liberal democracies are incapable of answering, inoculated as they are against the political possibilities of sacred narratives.

POLICING THE JEWISH AND CHRISTIAN MARTYRS

Jewish and Christian martyrs are subject to the same double policing. Depending though on how the relationship of Judaism with Christianity is described, one could speak of a double, triple, or even quadruple policing of the martyrs. Averting this complexity, however, it will be best at this point to parse out briefly the way in which both Jews and Christians, singly and

91. Ibid., 45.

together, are policed legitimately first among themselves and secondly and somewhat illegitimately from other perspectives. Such as with Islam, there are noticeably two arguments surrounding religious dying, one internal and the other external.

The origins of Jewish martyrdom lay in the conflict and assimilation with "Hellenistic influence" beginning in the third century before Christ[92] and culminating in the pagan erastianism of Antiochus Epiphanes IV.[93] Pagan temples and altars were built in villages outside Jerusalem in an effort to suppress the worship of Yahweh, provoking in effect a civil war between Jews who suffered and fought to remain faithful to Torah and those who were content to assimilate the terms of Seleucid domination.[94] The conflict was between the Jews of Jason and the Jews of Eleazar and Mattathias. Jason bought the high priesthood in Jerusalem and soon "shifted his compatriots over to the Greek way of life," introducing customs forbidden by Torah from what the Maccabean record describes as his boundless impiety.[95] Eleazar, however, refused to eat unlawful meat, spitting out the pork that had been forced into his mouth. Eleazar "went at once to the rack" and to his death, preferring to show his fidelity to Torah, not only to God but to the younger generations who would be influenced by his example.[96] Influenced they were, as 2 Maccabees immediately records the torture and execution of seven brothers and finally their mother.[97] Mattathias, in contrast, mourning that he should witness the ruin of his people and Jerusalem, and refusing to compromise his observance of Torah, responded differently. At Modein, when a Jew came forward to

92. Frend, *Martyrdom and Persecution*, 38.

93. Ibid., 41.

94. Ibid., 43.

95. 2 Macc 4:7–17.

96. Ibid., 6:18–30.

97. Ibid., 7:1–42.

offer unlawful sacrifice, Mattathias, as 1 Maccabees describes, "burned with zeal" and "gave vent to righteous anger" in killing the hapless Jew who had stepped forward.[98] Mattathias influenced his own younger generation, as the rest of 1 Maccabees records, to take up tumultuous armed revolution led by his son Judas and his brothers.

In both the stories of Eleazar and Mattathias, there are negotiations about the wisdom of particular forms of resistance, conflict, and dying that constitute the first legitimate policing of martyrdom within Judaism. Taking Eleazar aside, those overseeing the unlawful ritual meal suggested to him privately that he prepare and secretly bring his own kosher meat and "to pretend that he was eating the flesh of sacrificial meat that had been commanded by the king." Eleazar rejected this offer of escape. As 2 Maccabees describes it, his was a decision of "high resolve, worthy of his years." Eleazar defended his rejection of escape through charade: "Such pretense," he said,

> is not worthy of our time of life, for many of the young might suppose that Eleazar in his ninetieth year had gone over to an alien religion, and through my pretense, for the sake of living a brief moment longer, they would be led astray because of me, while I defile and disgrace my old age. Even if for the present I would avoid the punishment of mortals, yet whether I live or die I will not escape the hands of the Almighty. Therefore, by bravely giving up my life now, I will show myself worthy of my old age and leave to the young a noble example of how to die a good death willingly and nobly for the revered and holy laws.[99]

Mattathias reasoned differently. After the killing at Modein, Mattathias and his sons escaped into the hills. The story in

98. 1 Macc 2:7–28.

99. 2 Macc 6:21–28.

1 Maccabees immediately shifts to the desert where a large number of Jews had taken flight "because troubles pressed heavily upon them." A detachment of royal forces was sent to the desert after them, and after surrounding them and offering the king's idolatrous terms yet again, the Jews refused. The royal forces attacked, and since it was the Sabbath, the Jews offered no resistance. They were attacked on the Sabbath, "they died, with their wives and children and livestock, to the number of a thousand persons." For Mattathias the lesson of this massacre was clear:

> If we all do as our kindred have done and refuse to
> fight with the Gentiles for our lives and for our or-
> dinances, they will quickly destroy us from the earth
> . . . Let us fight against anyone who comes to attack
> us on the sabbath day; let us not all die as our kindred
> died in their hiding places.[100]

Mattathias and his sons decided then to join the Hasidim and to take up armed struggle. The stakes of negotiation between the forms of resistance exemplified by Eleazar and Mattathias were high. Both consciously courted death, but each with a different imagination. Eleazar appealed to the transcendent perspective of God, a divine gaze that neither he nor his torturers could escape, and so he was "glad to suffer."[101] Mattathias contemplated the annihilation of Torah and of his people, and so he and his comrades "rescued the law out of the hands of the Gentiles and kings, and they never let the sinner gain the upper hand."[102]

This Jewish argument between the merits and wisdom of either zealotry or passive martyrdom continued into the first century after Christ and beyond. Both Philo and Josephus

100. 1 Macc 2:28–41.
101. 2 Macc 6:30.
102. 1 Macc 2:48.

displayed a similar Maccabean ambivalence, admitting the validity of dying for Torah while criticizing rash violence and death.[103] Among the rabbis after the fall of Jerusalem in the first century, according to Frend, they "set to work to try to define more closely the situation when death was a necessity."[104] Daniel Boyarin suggests that this argument among the rabbis was carried on even centuries further, pointing to stories in the Babylonian Talmud valorizing both clever evasion as well as staunch, open resistance. The story of Rabbi Eli'ezer, for example, cleverly evading death by the double entendre of "I have trust in the judge" (meaning either God or the Roman judge)[105] is followed quickly by the story of Rabbi Hanina who was killed immediately upon answering the question "Why did you engage in Torah?" with "For thus the Lord my God has commanded me!"[106] This debate, never resolved in the Talmud, between the virtues of the evasive trickster or the noble martyr "was in the air as a living and active cross-confessional issue at the time that the talmudic literature was being composed."[107] As in 1 and 2 Maccabees, neither form of resistance exemplified by Mattathias and Eleazar is given priority in the Babylonian Talmud.

A similar (and perhaps even the same) argument is present among early Christians, although with finally less ambiguity.[108] Ignatius of Antioch, in his letter to the Trallians, exhibits both

103. Frend, *Martyrdom*, 53.

104. Ibid., 56.

105. Boyarin, *Dying for God*, 27.

106. Ibid., 56.

107. Ibid. For more on Boyarin's use of "trickster" language, see Scott, *Domination and the Arts of Resistance*, 162–66.

108. For a good discussion on the discursive development of martyrdom internal to Christianity, see Smith, "Martyrdom: Self-Denial or Self-Exaltation?" 169–96.

his own anxiety about his destined martyrdom as well as anxiety within his own community about his desired path. "God has certainly filled my head with a great many thoughts," Ignatius tells the Trallians, "but I am careful of my own limitations, for fear boasting should be the downfall of me." Ignatius tells of being scourged by the flattering words of his friends, some of whom had apparently tried to rescue Ignatius from his probable death. He ought, Ignatius thinks to himself, to have more humility and to disregard the sentiments of his friends.[109] To the Romans, Ignatius suggests that if they remain silent and not try to rescue him from death, he will become an "intelligible utterance of God," but if they only thought of his "poor human life" then he would "become a mere meaningless cry once more." He begs his friends: "suffer me to be a libation poured out to God, while there is still an altar ready for me."[110] A generation later the question of just what is an appropriate way to anticipate and court martyrdom is present in the account of Polycarp's martyrdom. Quintus the Phrygian is offered early as an example of a failed and impetuous martyr. He had worked himself and others up to surrender themselves but lost courage at the sight of the beasts, choosing at the last moment to take an oath and offer incense. There is an aside at this point in the account, making the lesson clear for the reader: "And that is the reason, brothers, why we do not approve of men offering themselves spontaneously. We are not taught anything of that kind in the Gospel."[111] Polycarp's several escapes, vision, arrest,

---

109. Ignatius of Antioch *Letter to the Trallians* 4.

110. Ignatius of Antioch *Letter to the Romans* 4. There is possibly an echo here of Acts 21:10–14 where Agabus's prophetical display provokes the people of Caesarea to urge Paul not go on to Jerusalem. Paul's response: "For I am ready not only to be bound but even to die in Jerusalem for the name of the Lord Jesus."

111. *Martyrdom of Polycarp* 4.

and death, in a rather gospel and liturgical pattern, appear almost as a correction to the rashness represented by Quintus and perhaps even by Ignatius. Thus by the end of the second century, the Lyons martyrs were those who had successfully trained and been properly coached in their confession.[112]

In North Africa over roughly the same period, similar questions were being raised about the motives and method of religious dying. Frend rather exaggerates differences,[113] but there do appear quite clearly contrasting ideas about martyrdom in Carthage and then in Alexandria in the late-second and early-third centuries. Tertullian, writing to the "Blessed Martyrs Designate" in prison, suggests that, for Christians, it is simply "the way of business to suffer present loss."[114] Writing decades later to the proconsul of Carthage, Tertullian offers that "it was ordained that we should suffer," suggesting "the greater our conflicts, the greater our rewards."[115] Admirably enumerating the noble deaths and suicides of pagan antiquity, Tertullian still judges these deaths to have been simply for false, earthly glory. The Christian martyrs, in contrast, die for truth. "Are we not called on, then," Tertullian concludes, "most joyfully to lay out as much for the true as others do for the false?"[116] In his letter to the proconsul, Tertullian shows that his conception of martyrdom has taken on a rather political zeal. Denying that

---

112. *Martyrs of Lyons* 1.11.

113. Frend, *Martyrdom and Persecution*, 361. There he muses that, "It is perhaps fortunate for the Church that Clement and Tertullian never met. If they had, or if the views of Clement and Origen had been propagated in Africa and Italy, the schism between East and West might have occurred in the third and not the eleventh century."

114. Tertullian *Ad Martyras* 1, 2.

115. Tertullian *To Scapula* 4.

116. Tertullian *Ad Martyras* 4.

Christians are enemies to Rome but are indeed beneficial,[117] as in the case of the Christian soldiers who prayed for rain in Marcus Aurelius' German campaign,[118] Tertullian argues that martyrdom has become a necessity so that Christians may set before the proconsul truths that he would not "listen to openly."[119] Martyrdom has become a powerful political option for Tertullian here, ending his letter to the proconsul with a very thinly veiled threat, asking:

> what will you make of so many thousands, of such a multitude of men and women, persons of every sex and every age and every rank, when they present themselves before you? How many fires, how many swords will be required? What will be the anguish of Carthage itself, which you will decimate, as each one recognizes there his relatives and companions, as he sees there it may be men of your own order, and noble ladies, and all the leading persons of the city, and either kinsman or friends of those of your own circle? Spare thyself, if not us poor Christians![120]

Is this martyrdom or mass suicide? The political threat makes all the difference. But what explains the zeal? For Tertullian, as Edward Malone argues, martyrdom—both spiritual and corporeal—was simply the only dutiful response to the threat of idolatry.[121] It was the only option for all Christians in the pagan world. Conflict and duty defined martyrdom for Tertullian.

In Alexandria the thinking was different. Whereas for Tertullian, martyrdom was understood as duty, for Clement martyrdom was more explicable as imitation and knowledge. In the

117. Tertullian *To Scapula* 2.
118. Ibid., 4.
119. Ibid., 1.
120. Ibid., 5.
121. Edward Malone, *Monk and Martyr*, 28.

Stromata, discussing martyrdom, Clement begins by describing the "perfect man." This is the ascetic philosopher of "gnostic alacrity" whose soul is in sufficient command of the body, so much so as "easily to be able to bear natural death, which is the dissolution of the chains which bind the soul to the body."[122] It is this essentially Stoic[123] habit that Clement baptizes, making it a criterion for what he calls a "gnostic" or "believing" martyr. Martyrdom, for Clement, is a "perfect work of love," which is to say that it is indeed a "voluntary" going to death but also an act of the will perfected in the knowledge of Christ. Proper knowledge is key to Clement's understanding of martyrdom. Only the true martyrs will know what should be done "for righteousness' sake" and will have "true desire." This knowledge, furthermore, is the fruit of imitating Christ. There are two ways (not mutually exclusive) of going about martyrdom for Clement, one christological and imitative, and one christological and mystical:

> We must then, according to my view, have recourse to the word of salvation neither from fear of punishment nor promise of a gift, but on account of the good itself. Such, as do so, stand on the right hand of the sanctuary; but those who think that by the gift of what is perishable they shall receive in exchange what belongs to immortality are in the parable of the two brothers called "hirelings." And is there not some light thrown here on the expression "in the likeness and image," in the fact that some live according to the likeness of Christ, while those who stand on the left hand live according to their image? There are then two things proceeding from the truth, one root lying beneath both,—the choice being, however, not equal, or rather the difference that is in the choice not being equal. To choose by way of imitation differs, as

122. Clement of Alexandria *Stromata* 4.3.

123. Ibid., 4.5.

> appears to me, from the choice of him who chooses
> according to knowledge, as that which is set on fire
> differs from that which is illuminated.[124]

Here Clement locates Christian martyrdom exclusively within a rather philosophical and tiered idea of Jesus discipleship. What distinguishes martyrdom from suicide is the imitation and knowledge of Christ, not even necessarily whether or not the martyr voluntarily went to her death. Like Tertullian, Clement recalls the noble deaths of pagan antiquity.[125] However, for him, it is an imitative and participatory knowledge of the Creator through Christ that marks the difference between suicide and martyrdom.[126] Thus, for Clement, martyrdom is not about the type of death or even the circumstances of its occasion. Rather, what constitutes martyrdom is the knowledge of Christ that makes for a true confession. Here Clement distinguishes between "confession" (*homologia*) and "defense" (*apologeisthai*). Everyone is called, following Luke 12:8, to confess Christ before the world, this being the testimony of the Spirit of the Father possible only in Christ. The "defense" of this confession, on the other hand, is entirely providential, for "that does not depend on us."[127] Clement by no means eliminates the good of physical martyrdom; rather, he locates physical death inside the spiritual and philosophical death of discipleship. What was for Tertullian a powerful political option was for Clement a mystical gift.

The argument over martyrdom goes on. Origen, Cyprian, Augustine, and Jerome, among others, each carry forward, amend, and revise the argument about what makes for martyrdom. Whether or not martyrdom was absorbed by monasticism,

124. Ibid., 4.6.
125. Ibid., 4.8.
126. Ibid., 4.4, 6.
127. Ibid., 4.9.

as Malone argues and Helen Rhee disputes,[128] is beyond this discussion—so are other questions like it. What is sufficient here is simply to point out, as the brief survey above shows, the first policing of Jewish and Christian martyrs. The above represents an essentially "in-house" debate about life and death, a discussion that among Christians, as will be argued later, is properly only explicitly and exclusively christological. At this point, however, it is necessary to point out the second policing of these martyrs.

There are quite literally countless books and articles dealing with Jewish and Christian martyrdom, although, in contrast to the literature treating Islamic martyrdom, this literature has the apparent air of history and mere academic distraction. This is only an illusion, for in the second policing of these martyrs is the assumption of the same liberal subjectivity at work in the discussions about Islam and suicide bombing. Different from the policing of Islamic martyrdom, however, is that whereas it is the ghost of liberal subjectivity that criticizes religious dying in Islam, in this literature the Jewish and Christian martyrs serve the myth of the formation of liberal subjectivity itself, martyrs apparently policing themselves. Taking Helen Rhee's suggestion of what are the three most influential works in this field, this discussion will proceed with the respective work of W. H. C. Frend, G. W. Bowersock, and Daniel Boyarin.[129]

Frend's 1965 *Martyrdom and Persecution in the Early Church* can be regarded as almost magisterial. The historical work and writing are remarkable. Beginning with a discussion of the account of the martyrdoms of Lyons in the late second century, Frend argues that there were strong ties between Jews and Christians there.[130] Pointing out also that the Lyons material

128. Rhee, *Early Christian Literature*, 193.

129. Ibid., 41–43.

130. Frend, *Martyrdom and Persecution*, 18.

"was saturated in Maccabean literature,"[131] Frend asks, "was there, after all, a deep and long-standing tradition of Christian thought which the martyrs represented and in the context of which their actions may be understood?"[132] The answer for Frend is clearly in the affirmative. There is, according to him, a "vital tradition"[133] stretching back deep into the history and psychology of Judaism. "Christ indeed had come on earth, had ministered, had suffered and died the true martyr," Frend begins his investigation, "but the idea of suffering and even death being involved in the act of witnessing to the power and the truth of God's Law goes far back in the Jewish religion."[134] Tracing a development that began from the time of Babylonian captivity to the Maccabean revolt, Frend argues that without "Maccabees and without Daniel a Christian theology of martyrdom would scarcely have been thinkable."[135] This history occasions what Frend calls the "Jewish psychology of martyrdom," features that strongly mark the differences between Jews and Gentiles and Palestinian and Diaspora Jews—these groups negotiating their identity through a theodicy of righteous suffering and cosmic history.[136] It is this specifically Jewish heritage that answers for Christian martyrdom. Of course, for Frend, Jesus Christ undoubtedly marks quite a significant development in this theology of martyrdom. Certainly Christ's suffering and sacrifice is only intelligible within the long Jewish tradition of martyrdom;[137]

131. Ibid., 20.
132. Ibid., 13.
133. Ibid., 14.
134. Ibid., 22.
135. Ibid., 65.
136. Ibid., 50.
137. Ibid., 81.

however, what Christ changes, according to Frend, is the scope of martyrdom. Enter in Frend's liberal subjectivity:

> Thus, it [Jewish nationalistic martyrdom] needed the life and death of Jesus to give a transcendent and universal application to the notion which had evolved in Judaism. Christianity as a religion which knew no boundaries of language or class, and which avoided the 'general fussiness of the Jews', could extend unequivocally the hope of individual blessedness for those who had borne witness to the reality of Christ's conquest of death. The early Christian fixed his eyes beyond this world in which he was a mere 'sojourner'. The Jew believed that Judaism would be the universal religion of mankind, and that all nations would ultimately be gathered in under the Old Dispensation. The claims of Judaism as a national religion clashed with its claims to be the religion of mankind. The Christian, living, and suffering and dying a witness to the Living Christ, believed that he was fulfilling the hopes which had inspired Old Israel since Maccabean times.[138]

What makes this a liberal subjectivity is not simply its supersessionism but, rather, its supersessionism located within a reconciling dialectic with the Roman Empire. The whole of Frend's momentous work seeks to identify the causes for the "triumph" of Christianity, naming obviously the events symbolized by the conversion of Constantine. What the Christian martyrs accomplished, according to Frend, was to present a political subjectivity free of the bonds of ethnicity and class with which the late Roman Empire had to negotiate. This "victory of Christianity," argues Frend, "accompanied other tendencies which amounted to a rejection of Classicism and a renewal of native, pre-Roman ways of life, which the decline of the city as the unit of culture and administration had allowed to emerge." In the displace-

138. Ibid., 68.

ment of power from urban to rural centers in the late third century "the Christian protest spread among populations which were prosperous and articulate enough to feel a sense of grievance and were prepared to break with their immediate past in order to express it."[139] Martyrdom for Frend, ultimately names a political subjectivity, as it should, yet in a recognizably liberal shape free of the claims of ethnic or sacramental kinship, both claims quickly giving way to the claims of the state.

In stark contrast to Frend's work, G. W. Bowersock's 1990 *Martyrdom and Rome* refutes any Semitic heritage at all for Christian martyrdom. Martyrdom in late antiquity "was not something that the ancient world had seen from the beginning." Surely there were "glorious examples of resistance to tyrannical authority," but "never before had such courage been absorbed into a conceptual system of posthumous recognition and anticipated reward."[140] For Bowersock, "there is no reason to think that anyone displayed anything comparable to martyrdom before the Christians."[141] The alleged Jewish heritage of martyrdom, according to Bowersock, was at best a construction contemporaneous with the emergence of Christian martyrdom "when the New Testament documents were coming into being and the zealous Ignatius was growing up."[142] Martyrdom, constitutively for Bowersock, "was constructed by the Christians in the hundred years or so between about 50 and 150."[143] What answers instead for Christian martyrdom is a particularly Graeco-Roman heritage:

> To put this in another way, Christianity owed its martyrs to the *mores* and structures of the Roman empire,

139. Ibid., 463.
140. Bowersock, *Martyrdom and Rome*, 5.
141. Ibid., 7.
142. Ibid., 12.
143. Ibid., 13.

> not to the indigenous character of the Semitic Near
> East where Christianity was born. The written record
> suggests that, like the very word "martyr" itself, martyr-
> dom had nothing to do with Judaism or with Palestine.
> It had everything to do with the Graeco-Roman world,
> its traditions, its language, and its cultural tastes.[144]

Bowersock reads the martyr acts within the tradition of the Greek novels[145] and the martyrs themselves in the tradition of the great sophists.[146] The martyrs, in their deaths, fit well within the Roman civic culture of valorized suicide[147] and gladiatorial spectacle.[148] Christian martyrdom "was anchored in a social and ceremonial context" that was itself undergoing a "reworking."[149] Here, the subjectivity Bowersock is defining is made clear. The martyr is one of several figures in early late antiquity to struggle for freedom. "This was an age," Bowersock contends, "in which philosophers as well as Christians stood up to the tyrannical authority of Rome and its emperor, even to the point of exile and death." Christian martyrs from this period represent one aspect of "a spreading desire for liberty and for freedom from the oppressor."[150] Again, as with Frend, martyrdom is read as an avenue leading to political liberty. The numerous historical arguments aside, both come to serve similar liberal subjectivities. As it will be argued below, this is not in itself the problem. The problem arises when the illegitimate policing commences, and when such a subjectivity is seen as all there is to explain martyrdom.

144. Ibid., 28.
145. Ibid., 24.
146. Ibid., 44.
147. Ibid., 72.
148. Ibid., 50.
149. Ibid., 55.
150. Ibid., 16.

Daniel Boyarin refreshingly complicates the arguments of both Frend and Bowersock. In his 1999 *Dying for God* Boyarin rescores his well-known argument that once Judaism and Christianity "were part of one complex family."[151] Boyarin pictures Judaism and Christianity upon a continuum, one end being occupied by Marcionites and the other by Jews "for whom Jesus meant nothing."[152] Understandably then, Frend and Bowersock come in for serious criticism. Both, according to Boyarin, assume *a priori* that "Judaism and Christianity are two separate entities, so that it is intelligible to speak of one (and not the other—either—one) as the point of origin of a given practice."[153] Bowersock's thesis that Christian martyrdom represents something entirely new is essentialist and dismissive of the complexity of the history involved.[154] Frend, on the other hand, is simply supersessionist. "He clearly wants to have his Jews and supersede them, too,"[155] Boyarin suggests, for by narrating Christian martyrdom as a development of Jewish martyrdom, Frend simply ruins the "historical specificity" both of the Maccabean crisis and of early Christians.[156]

Boyarin's thesis is deliberately hazy. For him martyrdom is simply a discourse, "a practice of dying for God and of talking about it."[157] Only in later discourse did certain deaths become martyrdoms[158] that served as emblems of thought resulting in "religious fecundity in both directions" in the construction

151. Boyarin, *Dying for God*, 6.

152. Ibid., 8.

153. Ibid., 93.

154. Ibid., 94.

155. Ibid., 129.

156. Ibid., 127.

157. Ibid., 94.

158. Ibid., 116.

of eventually separate Jewish and Christian orthodoxies.[159] Suggesting rabbinic and early Christian parallels, Boyarin argues that extreme antagonists in both Judaism and Christianity argued for strong and crisp identities, defined more firmly by either the *Shema* for Jews or the christological confession for Christians.[160] Both Jews and Christians for centuries, Boyarin would argue, were "never sure of their sovereign identity." Ultimately, however, Jewish and Christian identities would crystallize to the extent that ecclesiastically managed orthodoxies emerged.[161]

For Boyarin, unlike Frend and Bowersock, the liberal subjectivity at work is not really either the Jewish or Christian martyr (although Boyarin does not say either way if he thinks the martyr is an evolutionary species of liberalism); rather, the liberal subjectivity at work is Boyarin himself. Boyarin successfully and helpfully complicates earlier static narratives, and he astutely shows the problematic assumptions of his predecessors. However, in granting discourse analysis the final word, so to speak, Boyarin lurks, as Alasdair MacIntyre describes it, in the "shadow of self-congratulatory narrative."[162] This simulated post-subjectivity, as MacIntyre argues, is the very flaw of this type of genealogical work—the lie of postmodernity. Boyarin is most probably beyond the illusive liberalism seen in Frend's work; nonetheless, Boyarin's subjectivity issues from the same modern and postmodern font. Thus, insofar as Boyarin wears the interrogative mask of the genealogist, or as long as Frend and Bowersock describe martyrdom as a pre-modern expression of liberty, Jewish and Christian martyrdom is sufficiently policed and is rendered inappropriate for the present world.

159. Ibid., 101.

160. Ibid., 109.

161. Ibid., 6, 65.

162. MacIntyre, *Three Rival Versions of Moral Enquiry*, 209.

A YODERIAN DEMONOLOGY

The forgoing accounts of the second and illegitimate policing of the martyrs presuppose what John Milbank calls the "new metaphysics" of sociology's policing of the sublime.[163] From Dennett's and Harris's naturalistic reduction of sacred narratives to Cook's sociological and instrumental definitions of martyrdom as well as Khosrokhavar's psychological and political explanation of religious violence, and even to Frend's, Bowersock's, and Boyarin's re-narrations of martyrdom, and so on, the presupposition of a possible finite Kantian explanation rules. Milbank traces this new metaphysics from Durkheim and Weber's fundamental assumption of the reality of a given metaphysical superstructure called "society" and its basic relation to the "individual."[164] This is, simply, Milbank argues, a fundamental illusory perspective from which a given whole (i.e., society and individual) is seen and assessed. What this accomplishes is an artificial separation of the particular matrix immediately constructive of the concepts of society and individual. Likewise, this artificial conceptual separation belittles the necessary particularity of language and ritual in the reading of any given society. This inevitably reduces religion to something ephemeral and ultimately beyond regard.[165] This is the "remainder" to which theologians have too obediently turned their attention.[166] Theologians, according to Milbank, have too quickly assumed, following this new metaphysics, that religion must have an essence understood as "value"—a reified symbol-system that justifies the given society. This value is located either on the charismatic margins (Weber) or in some mysterious transcendence (Durkheim). In any case,

163. Milbank, *Theology and Social Theory*, 105.

164. Ibid., 102.

165. Ibid., 104.

166. Ibid., 101.

according to Milbank, it is all "locked into the paradox of the Kantian critique of metaphysics," assuming that "finite categories apply alone to the finite and are extended only illegitimately to the infinite."[167] Of course, maintaining this paradox requires at all times that two assumptions be upheld: first, one must maintain that an *a priori* division exists among concept and application and understanding (e.g., the classic arguments over causality); second, one must catalogue and mark the limits of all finite knowledge.[168] Assuming this basic Kantianism, religion can only be perceived, from the sociological gaze, "as belonging to the Kantian sublime."[169] Thus it is policed insofar as it is quarantined as an eccentricity with no real constitutive claim upon societies and individuals. Tracing this policing, Milbank describes several explanatory strategies, be they sacrificial, evolutionary, ideological, or so on, relating them to one of three sublimities, either ineffable, holistic, or transitional.[170] All policing, however, in effect abstracts religion for the social and manipulates it within its own symbolic structure that is ineluctably associated and monitored by the state.[171] Indeed, given this connection it is not difficult to see from this Harris's and Khosrokhavar's implication that what is really wrong with suicide bombing is not killing but rather non-state killing. If religion merely symbolizes the Kantian sublime and thus is in some sense unreal, then it must certainly be prevented from trading in the only real economy of violence.

What Milbank offers, from his place of "meta-suspicion," is none other than a demonology in the New Testament sense. And insofar as Milbank names the Kantian assumptions of

167. Ibid., 104.
168. Ibid., 105.
169. Ibid., 104.
170. Ibid., 109ff.
171. Ibid., 102.

sociological policing, he is in company with John Howard Yoder. Yoder's classic critique of H. Richard Niebuhr's *Christ and Culture* does much of the same work as Milbank's "meta-suspicion" and shows plainly that what is at stake for Christians is the recognition of demonic idolatry. Moreover, Yoder offers clues toward a recovery of Christian practices, such as martyrdom, that subvert these powers in the name of Jesus Christ.

Yoder's problem with *Christ and Culture* is not typology; rather, it is Niebuhr's poor use of typology. In rescoring two millennia of Christian thought, Niebuhr hoped to classify five basic types of Christians' relation to culture—Christ against, of, above, in paradox, and finally transforming culture. This typology was designed to shed light on the nature of the types classified. Aside from specific historical arguments about Niebuhr's assignments, Yoder argues that typology's helpfulness ought always to be reviewed. What are the claims being made by a typology? What is it trying to reveal? What might it be hiding?[172] The problem with Niebuhr's typology is that in reifying an abstract idea of culture Niebuhr was granting it an idolatrous monolithic autonomy that obscured the complexities of history and bullied past theologians.[173] Niebuhr's concept of culture, according to Yoder, is monolithic and autonomous in that he treats culture not only as a transcendent entity of human productivity consistently and holistically either rejected or accepted, but also because these norms constitute a single trans-historical universe of value. Thus, Jesus is evaluated against this abstract and universal standard.[174] Jesus, for Niebuhr, is therefore at best a moralist.[175] Although Jesus was certainly in a radical prophetic relationship to the world, his life and ministry, according to Niebuhr, must

172. Yoder, "How H. Richard Niebuhr Reasoned," 44.

173. Ibid., 45.

174. Ibid., 55.

175. Ibid., 59.

be assessed. Yoder's description of what Niebuhr's typology does to Jesus is succinct and to the point:

> Jesus has become in sum one of the poles of a dualism. It is we, the modern practitioners of Christian ethics, who shall judge to what extent we give our allegiance to him and to what extent we let his critical claims be conditioned by our acceptance of other values, within the culture, which He in principle calls us to turn away from. We also are in charge of defining the other pole of the dualism. We manage our epistemology. We are the moderators in charge of the balancing process. We want to be modest about this, but (according to Niebuhr) we still have the last word; Christ does not. Jesus is very important; Lord he is not, if "Lord" denotes an ultimate claim.[176]

As with Milbank's "meta-suspicion," policing sacred narratives and therefore policing the martyrs fundamentally assumes a narrative more determinative than that which the martyrs recognize themselves.[177] Thus, they are effectively subject to a hegemonic Kantian ridicule either secretly or explicitly associated with the state.[178] This is what Niebuhr's typology tacitly endorses; and for this reason, according to Yoder, it "becomes in the technical sense, demonic, a structure which gets in the way of wholeness and understanding rather than serving."[179]

If the task of policing the martyrs is to enforce a larger narrative upon the story of Israel, Jesus, and the Church, or upon the Prophet, the Qur'an, and the *Umma*, then it follows that in order to discover something approximating a genuine understanding of martyrdom, one should attend to the coherent

176. Ibid., 43.
177. Ibid., 46.
178. Ibid., 51, 55.
179. Ibid., 47.

stories of the martyrs themselves—by definition a subversive act. Simply, this is to listen *to the martyrs*, to believe them for a moment and to test the coherence of their claims within the horizon of the stories that have spoken these martyrs. To listen to the martyrs demands that the reader understand something of the nature of sacred stories and to allow herself to be, in some sense, vulnerable to these stories. That is, the reader must be willing to read stories while being open to the assumptions of sometimes alien narratives. Regarding the martyrs, the reader must ask what makes their suffering and death intelligible—not to the reader, but to the martyrs themselves.

A clue to figuring out how to begin to listen to the martyrs is found in the suggestion made by Stanley Hauerwas and Charles Pinches that it is possible to grasp that the stories of the martyrs are not about the martyrs but about God and the Church.[180] Since it is God who speaks salvation in the story of Israel and the Church, the martyr acts are therefore not stories of the same genre of Socrates's noble death. Rather, these stories are signifying moments within the story of Israel's redemption in Jesus and the Church.[181] Thus, neither the individual martyr nor the circumstances of her death constitute martyrdom; rather, it is the resurrection of Jesus Christ and his ascension to the right hand of the Father that makes certain deaths martyrdom. This is similar to Boyarin's notion of martyrdom as a discourse, yet here the discourse is located somewhere else. Just where this discourse is located is hinted at by Yoder and Samuel Wells. Toward the end of his critique of *Christ and Culture*, Yoder notes Niebuhr's failure to say much of anything about

---

180. Hauerwas and Pinches, *Christians Among the Virtues*, 161.

181. Samuel Wells makes much of Hauerwas and Pinches here. See his *Improvisation: The Drama of Christian Ethics*, 42–44. See also his "Disarming Virtue of Stanley Hauerwas," 82–88.

the Church.[182] What Yoder argues is necessary is a sociologically distinct fellowship of Christians that holds seriously to the idea of the incarnation, of a community that would struggle within the possibilities of the incarnation as if it were genuinely possible to act as if Jesus is indeed Lord. For Yoder this is a real and practicable process of community discernment, following its own canonical lines.[183] Wells understands this process to be primarily worship, wherein Christians find "their place and role in the story, of recognizing beginnings and endings, of seeing the author at work . . . of fitting their own small story into the large story of God."[184] Thus, in contrast to Boyarin, the discourse of martyrdom is not so hidden; rather, it is God's, and it is discovered in the Church of baptism and Eucharist.

Thus, it is only ecclesially that Christian martyrs' stories can be read. This is to say that it is only within the martyrs' own horizon of meaning that one can hope for a genuine hearing of the martyrs. This is not to subject the reader to the hegemony of the Church so much as to introduce the reader to the subject of the martyrs' witness. Clement of Alexandria suggested that martyrdom was about Jesus. Having named and renounced the powers, the next task to hand is to explore this suggestion.

182. Yoder, "How H. Richard Niebuhr Reasoned," 74.

183. Ibid., 77.

184. Wells, *Improvisation*, 82. See also, Hauerwas and Wells, "Christian Ethics as Informed Prayer," 3–12.

CHAPTER 2

I Am a Christian

MARTYRDOM AS OVERACCEPTANCE

"Who would doubt that death is a good?"

—Ambrose *Death as a Good* 9.38

MAKING SENSE OF SANCTUS

Sanctus said nothing to his torturers. He revealed nothing about his birthplace, his nationality, not even his name. He underwent horrific brutality, his abused body "being all one bruise and one wound, stretched and distorted out of any recognizably human shape." Throughout his torture, Sanctus answered none of the questions put to him. In response he only repeated in Latin, "I am a Christian."[1] It was sufficient that Sanctus's response, *Christianus sum*, stood for every other possible explanation and reason that could have brought Sanctus to this apparently brutal moment. If it is the case, as the first chapter argues, that Christian martyrdom properly described has something to do with Jesus, then Sanctus's response represents something basic to every Christian martyrdom. In order

1. *The Martyrs of Lyons* 1.21.

to give an account of Christian martyrdom that refuses to police ways of dying deemed illegitimate by liberal secular politics, it is necessary to explore the narrative imagination of the martyrs themselves. That is, Sanctus's response to his torturers will continue to mystify those who refuse to explore the discursive world of the people for whom this response was adequate. Those who encounter the stories of the martyrs are continually invited to do just that. Thus, the purpose of this chapter is to explore the narrative and theological imagination of the martyrs of Lyons and Vienne. As representatives, from their witness, it will be possible to discover the christological place and moment wherein the martyrs confessed their faith—a moment at once small in its existential and historical display and also infinitely broad in its eschatological hope and sacrificial patience.

What one discovers in the account of the martyrdoms of Lyons and Vienne is a rather plaited narrative of intersecting stories brought to fulfillment in the repeated martyrs' confessions that they are Christians. Early in the account there is a contrast made between making a "confession" (*homologia*) of faith and an "apology" (*apologoumenos*) for the "brethren." Vettius Epagathus loved both God and his neighbor, and he desired to rebut the false accusations of atheism and impiety. However, the circumstances were never amenable for him to make a defense: "Although he was a distinguished person the crowd around the tribunal shouted him down. The prefect dismissed the just request that he had put forward and merely asked him if he too were a Christian." The clamor and noise of the tribunal were quieted by the pointed question posed by the prefect leading to an equally direct response when Vettius "admitted in the clearest tones" that he was a Christian. The story is brought to an abrupt conclusion, recording only that "he too was accepted into the ranks of the martyrs." The suggestion being made is that Vettius's simple confession was better than his initial designs to defend the

Christians' innocence. In ranking Vettius with the martyrs, the author identifies him with Zechariah, John the Baptist's father, who likewise was confounded in his own power of speech until compelled by the Spirit.[2] There is here in the opening scene of this martyr account a redefinition and redemption of advocacy that is repeated throughout the remaining letter. The author does not reject *tôn adelphôn apologias* outright; rather, in the story of Vettius the very character of that defense is reshaped.[3]

The story of Vettius sets the stage for the numerous martyrdoms that follow in the account, most of them culminating in a confession of faith that was expressed by Sanctus, Blandina, and others in the words "I am a Christian." Such an expression was the summit of the martyr's action as well as an entrance into a different way of suffering. During her torture, Blandina "got renewed strength with her confession of faith: her admission, 'I am a Christian; we do nothing to be ashamed of,' brought her refreshment, rest, and insensibility to her present pain."[4] Likewise, Sanctus, "cooled and strengthened" by his confession of faith, appeared in the amphitheater for a second round of torture, but,

> to the men's complete amazement, his body unbent and became straight under the subsequent tortures; he recovered his former appearance and the use of his limbs. Indeed, the second trial by the grace of Christ proved to be not a torture but rather a cure.[5]

Even the aspect of the martyrs is said to have become more beautiful after their confessions in contrast to the ugliness of those who failed in theirs:

2. Luke 1:22.
3. *Martyrs of Lyons* 1.9–10.
4. Ibid., 1.19.
5. Ibid., 1.24.

> The former advanced joyously, with majesty and
> great beauty mingled on their countenances, so that
> even their chains were worn on them like some lovely
> ornament, as for a bride adorned with golden embroi-
> dered tassels, exhaling at the same time the sweet odor
> of Christ, so that some thought they had anointed
> themselves with a perfume of this world. But the oth-
> ers were dejected, downcast, ill-favored, and devoid
> of all comeliness.[6]

These were the "finest" of Christians, the "most zealous Christians of the two communities and those on whom everything
depended." Their arrests aroused fear not only for the extinc-
tion of the community but also "that some might fall away" and
bring shame to the church.[7] Yet even those who faltered were
reintegrated into the company of those who had made a good
confession—unless they "had never enjoyed even a vestige of
the faith nor any knowledge of *the wedding garment*," those who
were apparently the destined "sons of perdition."[8] The "stillborn," those who had failed to make a good confession upon
their arrest, were given another opportunity to confess the faith
by "a great divine favour, and the boundless mercy of Jesus"
that was "still not beyond the art of Christ."[9] These, "dead,"
were brought back to life by the mercy and mediation of those
who had not faltered; through the martyrs, the stillborn "were
conceived and quickened again in the womb and learned to
confess Christ"[10]; the devil being "forced to disgorge alive all
those whom he at first thought he had devoured."[11]

6. Ibid., 1.35. See also Acts 6:15.

7. Ibid., 1.12.

8. Ibid., 1.48.

9. Ibid., 1.32.

10. Ibid., 1.46.

11. Ibid., 2.6.

Among the more notable figures of the account, especially Sanctus, Pothinus, and Blandina, there is an explicit identification with Christ in their sufferings. For Sanctus, it was "Christ suffering in him"[12] who enabled him to overcome his torture. The crowds shouted at the elderly Pothinus "as though he were Christ himself."[13] Blandina, more spectacularly than the others, resembled Christ in her suffering:

> She seemed to hang there in the form of a cross, and by her fervent prayer she aroused intense enthusiasm in those who were undergoing their ordeal, for in their torment with their physical eyes they saw in the person of their sister him who was crucified for them, that he might convince all who believe in him that all who suffer for Christ's glory will have eternal fellowship in the living God.[14]

Blandina, figured at once as the mother in 2 Maccabees 7, as Christ, and as the Church, achieved in "her intimacy with Christ" an unprecedented status, suffering as "no woman had ever suffered" in her death. The consummation of many of the martyrs' sufferings is explicitly described as a sacrifice, Blandina finally being "offered in sacrifice" like Christ.[15]

Such, in brief outline, are some of the characteristics of those who made a good confession in Lyons. Many of these features will be revisited and explored further below. At this point, however, it is worthwhile to wonder just what explains the difference it made for Sanctus, Blandina, and the others to say, "I am a Christian." The statement by itself is enigmatic; it points to another world, the hope for which these martyrs were

12. Ibid., 1.23.
13. Ibid., 1.30.
14. Ibid., 1.41.
15. Ibid., 1.56.

content to suffer in this one. It is a deliberately leading statement, at once intended to explain the reality of the moment and
to connect that person and moment to some more meaningful
universe than the one in which they are suffering. Robin Young
does well to point to the larger imagination expressed in this
account, to an "entire cosmos filled with the forces of God and
the forces of Satan."[16] Young sees the Lyons account and others
in terms of an irresolvable conflict between Christian *ritus* and
Roman *mos maiorum*:

> The martyrs knew well what they were dealing with.
> They were opposing their sacrifices to the sacrifices of
> the local and universal cults of Rome, and opposing
> their visions of true imperium, derived from Jewish
> scripture, to the accepted order of those who ruled the
> Mediterranean and surrounding lands.[17]

Martyrdom, according to Young, was a liturgical catechesis in a
time when the Eucharist was guarded from non-believers.[18] For
her, these martyrdoms were deliberately liturgical, bringing the
sacrifice of Jesus to bear on the sacrifices of pagan Rome:

> All of the above—the careful presentation of confes-
> sion, the substitution of the martyrs' sacrifice for the
> pagan ceremony, and the conquest of that ceremony
> by the agents of Christ—all of it was performed by
> those whose preparation for the contest and encoun-
> ter with it resembled what they would have done for
> a ritual. Because it was indeed a ritual of sacrifice
> performed in front of an audience of the potential
> catechumens and because its object was the conver-

16. Young, *In Procession Before the World*, 35.
17. Ibid., 8.
18. Ibid., 12.

sion of the world, this performance took on more and
more the character of a liturgical ritual.[19]

Undoubtedly, this is correct. However, there is much more than
can be said here. For the rediscovery of Christian martyrdom as
something other than the deadly apogee of faith as it is widely
assumed to be, the enigmatic *Christiana sum* welcomes a richer
theological conversation than is provided by Young. She is
certainly right to suggest that martyrdom in this period was a
quasi-liturgical performance meant to convert the world, but in
order to understand martyrdom genuinely as something even
beyond the conflict between "two distinct societies' divergent
sacrificial systems,"[20] an even broader theological horizon must
be found. Something is necessarily missing from an account of
martyrdom that is content simply to delineate the battle lines of
the martyrs' conflict. There is something more to the martyrs'
actions that understands their suffering and death not as com-
petitive and irresolvable but, more importantly, as redemptive
and reconciling.

NO SACRED EGOISM

In trying to make sense of Sanctus and the other martyrs of
Lyons, Robin Young's suggestion that martyrdom be read li-
turgically offers a much better understanding of Christian
martyrdom than is put forward by those who refuse to grant le-
gitimacy to Christian narrative imagination. However, Young's
description of martyrdom falls short to the extent that she does
not explore the possible christological vocation genetic in the
martyrs' confessions. The picture one is left with in Young's account is of an irresolvable conflict involving the politics and

19. Ibid., 37.
20. Ibid., 1.

cosmos of the Roman world of late antiquity and the world of Jews and Christians. Such a conflict was undoubtedly real, as the numerous martyrs' stories show. Nonetheless, if such conflict was permitted the last word in describing the martyrs' actions, then there would be little to say about the uniqueness or, more importantly, about the peaceableness, of Christian martyrdom. Karl Barth is helpful here in that he locates the conflict Young describes not in terms of competing sacrificial systems but rather christologically and existentially, explicitly as part of a much larger christological vocation. Beginning with a theological description of the Christian person, Barth makes a more comprehensive understanding of martyrdom possible and offers a way of reading martyrdom that ultimately reconciles instead of rejects the world.

For Barth, the Christian person is she "whom Jesus Christ has called to attachment to Himself, to His discipleship and to living fellowship with Himself, and whom, as we finally say, He has bound and indeed conjoined with Himself."[21] Fundamentally this creates a distinction between those "who exist at the side of God who acts and reveals Himself in Jesus Christ" and those who do not. Moreover, these distinct persons attached to Christ act in some way in conjunction with the revelation of God in Christ. "The God who has reconciled the world to Himself is not alone as the true Witness and Proclaimer of this event."[22] Here the question emerges for Barth whether or not "the being of the Christian may be centrally represented in terms of this dialectic of worldliness and unworldliness and therefore of eschatological tension."[23]

21. Barth, *Church Dogmatics* IV/3.2, 555.

22. Ibid., 557.

23. Ibid., 558.

This is a risky question, Barth thinks, for there is a tendency, often repeated in history, to view the Christian and non-Christian dialectic in Kantian terms. That is, the unique principle of Christian existence is often conceived in abstraction as an "ethos" encompassing some sort of system of "self-glorifying Christian moralism" dangerously identified throughout history with particular manifestations of power and cultural chauvinism. Further, Barth argues, when the principle of Christian existence is thought of in terms of ethos, the result is always a "relativising and leveling down of the difference between Christian and non-Christian existence," for there emerges the necessity to manufacture a Kantian conceptual norm to delineate the Christian ethos.[24] This is precisely the danger that Young's account does not avoid, her thesis portraying only a politically and cosmically conflicted world devoid of any real suggestion as to why so many Christians in late antiquity were willing to suffer and die in so many spectacular and varied ways.

Avoiding this rather Nietzschean trap, Barth, in contrast, removes the question of Christian existence from abstraction:

> The Christian ethos does not allow itself to be understood as an end in itself. It is not a first thing, but follows from what Jesus Christ and Christians, what He commands and they who obey, are in themselves and in their mutual relationship prior to their commanding and obedience.[25]

That is, while the Christian ethos "is indispensable in its own place," the unique principle of Christian existence is not at first anything conceptual. Rather, Christian existence is first and foremost a vocation. Whatever may be conceptually established

24. Ibid., 559.
25. Ibid., 560.

regarding Christian existence, for Barth, is always *a posteriori* to the task implied in vocation.

Of course, simply talking about vocation in favor of ethos does not remove every danger. Indeed, there seem to be as many possibilities for deception and arrogance as before. Turning from an examination of ethos to vocation, Barth analyzes what he calls the "classic" answer for what marks the Christian off from the world, namely that,

> there can surely be nothing more obvious than to
> define the Christian as the man who is distinguished
> from others by the address, reception, possession, use
> and enjoyment of the salvation of God given and re-
> vealed to the world by God in Jesus Christ.[26]

This is a very individualistic view of vocation, one that em- phasizes the Christian's relationship with the Father in Christ as liberation from the travail of the world. "What could be more relevant than that which in supreme and ultimate mat- ters concerns me?"[27] Such has been the question often drawn, "and not by the worst people."[28] Yet to this Barth asks quite a postmodern question:

> And does he [the Christian] not sometimes come
> across non-Christians—pious Hindus or Buddhists,
> or the valiant, cheerful and often very serious children
> of the world whom we often meet in the West—who
> do not merely say but demonstrate in astonishing
> fashion that even without the benefit of Jesus Christ,
> and in a very different language, conceptuality and
> terminology, that have something analogous to or
> even identical with his Christian being, possession
> and capacity, namely, that they are not strangers to,

26. Ibid., 561.

27. Ibid., 563.

28. Ibid., 564.

but enjoy to an astonishing degree, something of the same peace and patience and trust and discipline and freedom in and in face of the world?[29]

The obvious health and peaceableness of so many who do not share in the *beneficia Christi* is enough for Barth to argue, as with his argument against Christian ethos, that the classic description of Christian vocation in overly individualistic evangelical terms fails in that it is too often seen as a sacred status that is grounded in itself. The consequence of this is what Barth calls *sacro egoismo*. Barth asks, "Does not this wholly possessive being seem to smack of the sanctioning and cultivating of an egocentricity which is only too human for all its sanctity, of a self-seeking which in the light of what is at stake renders every other form of self-seeking innocuous?"[30]

Because of these egotistical hazards Barth simply rejects the claim that either the Christian ethos or the "classic" answer of individual vocation sufficiently articulates the principle of Christian existence. For him, Christian existence cannot be grounded "directly or in itself"; rather, it must be "grounded indirectly."[31] Christian existence must be received from beyond its own parameters. Barth does not completely refuse ethos or the *beneficia Christi*; he simply refuses them any constitutive role in the description of Christian existence.[32]

It is here that Barth begins to construct a biblical doctrine of vocation in his characteristically exhaustive fashion. Nowhere, he argues, in the Old or New Testaments is the "classic" answer made "the true point and meaning of the distinction of the

29. Ibid., 565.
30. Ibid., 567.
31. Ibid., 566.
32. Ibid., 571.

called."[33] Rather, those who are called are simply those persons
who have been given something to do. The called are those who
have been given a task, and existence is constitutive in the execution of that task and in nothing more:

> The true substance of their standing, that which dis-
> tinguishes them decisively from others as the called,
> consists absolutely in their existence in execution of
> the task which God has laid upon them. This makes
> them what they are. Their personal being, possession
> and capacity, the honour, joy, assistance, comfort
> and encouragement, the whole exaltation which they
> themselves enjoy as this task is given them and they
> can and should execute it, all these constitute the
> indispensable periphery which is not actually with-
> held from them. But the task is the centre of their
> existence.[34]

The origin of this task is utterly extrinsic to those who are called.
They are witnesses, not directly of God's being "in His hidden
Godhead." Rather, they are primarily witnesses "of His being in
His past, present and future action in the world and in history,
of His being in His acts among and upon men." This witness
is explicitly, therefore, to Jesus "as God with us, Emmanuel,
was, is and will be with His creation, the world and all men."[35]
Thus Barth understands Christian existence constitutively only
to be the ministry of the divine Word. "They are *Verbi divini
ministri*."[36] In the concluding footnotes of this subsection of the
Dogmatics, Barth is most explicit:

> He does not bear witness abstractly to benefits and
> gifts which he may point out to those around as one

33. Ibid., 573.
34. Ibid., 575.
35. Ibid.
36. Ibid., 576.

who knows and has received them, but concretely to Jesus as the Lord, the Son of God, the Messiah, the Saviour of the world, in short, as the Subject, source and fulness of the grace which God has manifested to the world and all men and which includes as such all the benefits and gifts which may be seriously regarded as such.[37]

Simply, for Barth, the existence of the Christian is only her pointing, indication, and witness to Jesus. No prior description of the Christian is possible.

Bringing the discussion back to martyrdom, and in contrast to Robin Young's account of Christian martyrdom, it is possible to mark the difference Barth makes in the rediscovery of Christian martyrdom as something unique and peaceable. For Barth, that the principle of the Christian's existence is that she is fundamentally always a witness to Jesus means that the Christian is always a person involved in the world. The Christian witness does not point to God as does a philosopher to some Timean deity; rather, the Christian witnesses to the activity of God in history—past, present, and future. The Christian renders her service "in and to the world,"[38] not merely within a cosmic revolution but more significantly within a cosmic reconciliation:

> But the principle which controls the structure of his existence as one who is called is that God on the one side and the world and his fellows on the other have become more important to him and indeed qualitatively more important, than he can be to himself . . . As a witness of this kind he may confidently let well alone and things will definitely go well with him. Basically and finally all things will work together for

37. Ibid., 614.
38. Ibid., 576.

> good to him both in time and eternity . . . As such
> he stands under the command to love God and his
> neighbor, in which there is no question of self-love,
> even the highest and finest. His regard must be first for
> the kingdom, i.e., the establishment of the lordship of
> God in the world and the righteousness of this king-
> dom, i.e., what is right in the light of its coming. This
> regard is the principle which controls him. Caught up
> in it, he may rest assured that "all these things," both
> small and great, will be added to him.[39]

Unlike Young's account that takes what is essentially the classical and imperial Roman view that Christianity genuinely
was a *religio illicita* in total conflict with the *mos maiorum*,
Barth provides a way of reading early Christian martyrdoms as
radical moments of reconciliation instead of as skirmishes in
a Mediterranean clash of civilizations. Simply, Barth makes it
possible to read Christian martyrdom as peace:

> We come nearer to the heart of the matter when we
> go on to say that the action in fulfillment of which
> Christ and the Christians are one, He proceeding in
> His own way and the Christian following in his, takes
> place in a great context as part of the history of salva-
> tion, of the history of God in and with the world, in
> which the point at issue is the divinely willed and ac-
> complished renewal, restoration and fulfillment of the
> covenant which He made with the world in creating
> it, the irruption, dawn and lordship of His glory in it,
> and therefore its deliverance, salvation and peace. The
> starting-point common to Christ and the Christian
> is the will of the gracious and merciful God as a true
> Creator and omnipotent Reconciler.[40]

39. Ibid., 593.
40. Ibid., 598.

That the Christian is a witness to Jesus in the world is the larger dynamic iterated in the confession "I am a Christian." The tension between the Christian martyrs and the pagan world is more than an irredeemable conflict between cultures and civilizations. If Barth's doctrine of vocation is allowed as a commentary on the confession common to the martyrs, then it is possible to suggest that early Christian martyrs were not zealous ideologues facing impossible opposition in a Roman world that had to be confronted and destroyed in order to be made Christian. Rather, Barth's theology allows martyrdom to be read not only as liturgy, as with Young, but more significantly as peace. Eusebius called the martyrdoms of Gaul the "peaceful wars."[41] Barth shows how this could be more than mere rhetorical piety.

MAKING USE OF DEATH

Understanding something of the confession *Christiana sum*, it remains unclear just what role death played in early Christian martyrdoms. The Lyons account simply repeats that these martyrs "were in the end sacrificed," offering only that, as with Blandina, they saw in her "him who was crucified for them, that he might convince all who believe in him that all who suffer for Christ's glory will have eternal fellowship with God."[42] But what does this suggest? Why was death the "happy ending" as Judith Perkins describes it? How does death allow the hero to be replaced by the martyr in early Christian discourse? Numerous explanations have been offered describing Christian martyrdom as a sort of discursive revolution, again reading the conflict as basically an ideological one. These explanations are at best only half true, but they finally give way not to an ideology but to a

41. Eusebius *History of the Church* 5.1.
42. *Martyrs of Lyons* 1.41.

reconciling theological doxology found in the New Testament: "Where, O death, is your victory? Where, O death, is your sting?"[43]

Judith Perkins, for example, locates the early martyr accounts within a larger "representational revolution"[44] within Christian discourse in which the self was reconstituted as sufferer. All that contemporary pagans knew of early Christianity, Perkins suggests, was "that Christians held death in contempt and were ready to suffer for their beliefs."[45] Death in early Christian discourse was a "happy ending," rivaling the classical "conventional literary happy ending" of marriage and patriarchy.[46] Thus death in the budding discursive tradition of martyr accounts, apocryphal acts, and even the apologies[47] produced and represented a subversive element within early Christianity. Perkins argues that Christians presented themselves as sufferers for just such a subversive end. In these early texts Perkins suggests that there is an ongoing "self-fashioning"[48] of Christian subjectivity that "projects a subversion of the contemporary hierarchy through the power acquired by suffering."[49] This subversion is encoded in the portrayal of suffering and death and even in the eschatology present in early texts. Belief in the resurrection of the body and of the final judgment, for example, simply extend the contemporary material and political conflict beyond the moment of death, refusing rather dramatically the present configuration of Roman power while hoping for an

43. 1 Cor 15:55.

44. Perkins, *Suffering Self*, 17.

45. Ibid., 18.

46. Ibid., 26.

47. Ibid., 31.

48. Ibid., 104.

49. Ibid., 113.

identical yet reversed relationship of power beyond death.[50] That Christianity constructed a suffering subjectivity is not, in Perkins's view, an exaltation of some idea of the victim;[51] rather, it is a powerful challenge to the traditional discourse of power in late antiquity.[52]

Perkins's argument that early Christianity manufactured the new subjectivity of "sufferer," somewhat similarly to other contemporaneous discourses,[53] and that this new subjectivity rivaled more classical and offensive forms of power, fits comfortably within the familiar trope of *ressentiment*. Like Young's treatment of martyrdom, in one sense her argument clarifies the complex social tensions involved in the discursive and real conflicts between early Christians and others in late antiquity. However, in another very important way her argument occludes what Barth called the "principle of Christian existence" operating within early Christian discourse. Perkins would not allow such a Barthian critique, of course, as it would be beyond the scope of her discussion. But without such a discussion, her description of Christian subjectivity runs the risk of being simply a static, anachronistic, unreal tautology. For Perkins, to use a Barthian critique, the question of subjectivity is problematically located before the question of vocation; or more precisely, the Barthian question of vocation and subjectivity is replaced by the question of subjectivity and power. This makes for a tautological reduction in describing early Christians. According to Perkins, early Christians "had use for adversity, for the suffering of sickness, loss, or persecution, and could accept these within the context

50. Ibid., 122.
51. Ibid., 111.
52. Ibid., 115.
53. Ibid., 199.

of their belief that to be a Christian was to suffer."[54] No other use of suffering is intelligible for Perkins other than for making a certain sort of self, and this inexplicably suffering self allows no more description than to say that the Christian is a sufferer because to be a Christian is to be a sufferer. Any deeper read of early Christianity, for Perkins, can only understand Christian subjectivity as a certain form of power (the power of the sufferer) as is every other formation of the self. This is a variation on what Barth critically dubbed the "classical answer" of Christian existence, a distinction rendered no longer "by the address, reception, possession, use and enjoyment of the salvation of God given and revealed to the world by God in Jesus Christ,"[55] but now by a certain branding of power gradually finding currency in late antiquity in a rather Hobbesian metaphysics of power assumed to be universal and timeless in Perkins's argument. Her description of early Christians is pre-programmed, so to speak, by what she believes to be true about power—that it can only be coveted and never properly used. Thus, for Perkins, she can go no further in describing early Christianity than her rather sophisticated but superficial initial read of the extant literature.

Talal Asad helps clarify Perkins's description of the Christian self as sufferer by talking about passivity and agency. Asad rejects what he understands to be the modern secular dichotomy of the agent and the victim (the former "representing and asserting himself or herself" and the latter "the passive object of chance or cruelty").[56] Perkins would undoubtedly reject this as well; for according to both, the passive and suffering self can also be an agent. However, following cues from Wittgenstein,[57] Asad is

---

54. Ibid., 39.

55. Barth, *Church Dogmatics* IV/3.2, 561.

56. Asad, *Formations of the Secular*, 79.

57. Ibid., 81.

able to enliven Perkins's account of the suffering self by contextualizing that subjectivity within a nexus of relationships, which are in part produced and sustained by that same subjectivity:

> An agent suffers because of the pain of someone she loves—a mother, say, confronted by her wounded child. That suffering is a condition of her relationship, something that includes her ability to respond sympathetically to the pain of the original sufferer. The person who suffers because of another's pain doesn't first assess the evidence presented to her and then decide on whether or how to react. She lives in a relationship. The other's hurt—expressed in painful words, cries, gestures, unusual silences (in short, a recognizable rhetoric)—makes a difference to her in the sense of being the active reason for her own compassion and for her reaching out to the other's pain. It is a practical condition of who she and her suffering child are.[58]

For Asad, experiences of pain "are not simply mediated culturally and physically, *they are themselves modes of relationship*."[59] The point here is that relationships render the experience of pain in the suffering self agentive and no longer just passive. The experience of pain becomes the way the self relates to the world beyond itself. Perkins argues the same, but Asad's emphasis on pain as a mode of relationship gives a nuance to Perkins's description of subjectivity not found in her own arguments. Whereas Perkins emphasizes the Christian self's tension with the late antique world as an ideological one, Asad's description of the agentive sufferer opens up the possibility of seeing early Christian subjectivity aesthetically. For early Christian martyrs, "their suffering made a difference not only to themselves (to

58. Ibid., 82.

59. Ibid., 84 (Asad's emphasis).

their own potential actions) as members of a new faith but also to the world in which they lived: it required that one's own pain and the pain of others be engaged with differently."[60] Moreover, for Asad, pain not only "reproduces and sustains human relationships"[61] but in so doing it also creates the "epistemological status of 'the body.'"[62] Thus, for the Christian martyrs, the experience of suffering and death was not just the consequence of a certain realization of subjectivity; it was the aesthetic recreation of the human person and of the world.

Asad's discussion of the passive agent brings the discussion of the role of death in Christian martyrdom directly into theological considerations. To begin, it is helpful to follow Asad's suggestion that the suffering person is indeed agentive and that such agency is itself constitutive and productive of the relationships in which such pain is intelligible. This is a deeply theological insight present in the earliest stories of Jews and Christians. Pain marks the disobedient relationships of the first man and woman—with each other, with God, and with creation.[63] In the New Testament, Paul enigmatically told the Corinthians that in him "death is at work" so that the life of Jesus might be made visible.[64] But what makes pain and death relational? How, then, is death useful? As the rest of this section will argue, the clarification of Asad's intuition relating to Christian martyrdom is a theological task—a project that unites the role of death with the confession of the martyr in a singly performed moment when death becomes, as Maximus the Confessor says, "the 'father' of everlasting life."[65]

60. Ibid., 87.
61. Ibid., 88.
62. Ibid., 92.
63. Gen 3:16–19.
64. 2 Cor 4:10–12.
65. Maximus the Confessor *Ad Thalassium* 61.93.

Reflection upon how things and people are used (*uti*) in relation to how they are enjoyed (*frui*) long precedes Christian moral thought. Likewise, thinking about the value and role of death, the existence of the soul and its immortality is doubly primeval. Pain and pleasure in the *Phaedo*, for example, work together, "nailing" the soul to the body in revolving bodily extremes.[66] The practice of philosophy, therefore, is "to practice for dying and death."[67] The liberation that death facilitates however is prepared only by the immortal soul's orientation to the eternal forms: to the Just, the Beautiful, the Good, and so on.[68] True knowledge, knowing the forms, is achieved only after death, for "it is impossible to attain any pure knowledge with the body."[69] However, bodily life prior to death, if it is philosophical, is itself aesthetic in that it describes whatever is beautiful only in recognizing its participation in Beauty itself.[70] It is within this aesthetic economy that pain and pleasure are valued and in which death is read as the mode of return from the imperfectly beautiful to Beauty.

In Christian thought, Augustine describes this basic tension of *exitus/reditus* and its economy of pain, pleasure, and death in explicitly christological terms. For him the soul does not initially focus upon the eternal forms but first upon Christ. In *De Trinitate* Christ is, for Augustine, the divine-visible who deigned to be "originated" for the sake of an encounter with fallen humanity. As Augustine describes it, God sent his son as a man to "capture our faith."[71] Christ, and not the immaterial forms, is the person upon whom the person, body and soul, sets

66. Plato *Phaedo* 60b, 83c–d.

67. Ibid., 64a.

68. Ibid., 65d.

69. Ibid., 66e.

70. Ibid., 100d.

71. Augustine *The Trinity* 4.4.24.

her gaze. The mind is still meant, "once purified, to contemplate eternal things," yet while the mind is still undergoing purification, it must "give faith to temporal things." In *De Trinitate* faith pertains to "things done in time for our sakes" and to "what we are promised as believers."[72] These "things" refer to the biblical story, the encounter with which presents Christ who is the object of love.

The effect of this unique trinitarian mission is traced out more thoroughly in *De Doctrina Christiana*. There, in the first book, Augustine makes explicit the trinitarian and christological focus for the returning soul:

> The things therefore that are to be enjoyed are the Father and the Son and the Holy Spirit, in fact the Trinity, one supreme thing, and one which is shared in common by all who enjoy it; if that is to say, it is a thing, and not the cause of all things; if indeed it is a cause.[73]

Likewise, as in *De Trinitate*, it is Christ through whom trinitarian enjoyment is facilitated because humans would be unable to enjoy the ineffable Trinity "unless Wisdom herself had seen fit to adapt herself even to such infirmity as ours, and had given us an example of how to live, in no other mode than the human one, because we too are human."[74] As the rest of *De Doctrina Christiana* describes, the incarnation is itself an aesthetic revolution that reorders loves and knowledges so that the person encountering Christ in Scripture can be trained in ways of loving and knowing in order to love as Christ does, that is, loving enemies in peace.

72. Ibid.

73. Augustine *Teaching Christianity* 1.5.5.

74. Ibid., 1.11.11.

The "return home," according to Augustine, is not a journey "from place to place, but one traveled by the affections." It is not just that Augustine biblically re-narrates a Platonic pattern that makes sense of his use of *uti*-love and *frui*-love. Rather, that which completes the rehabilitation, so to speak, of the *uti/frui* distinction is Christ. It is remarkable that in so much that is written on Augustine's use of the *uti/frui* distinction, little is made of the fact that crucial to Augustine's use of the distinction is the exemplary role of Jesus Christ as he is biblically presented. The fundamental distinction between *uti*-love and *frui*-love at work in *De Doctrina Christiana* is essentially a reflection of Christology, in that it is Christ the mediator who serves as the principle model for the ordering of love:

> Furthermore, we are still on the way, a way however not from place to place, but one traveled by the affections. And it was being blocked, as by a barricade of thorn bushes, by the malice of our past sins. So what greater generosity and compassion could he show, after deliberately making himself the pavement under our feet along which we could return home, than to forgive us all our sins once we had turned back to him, and by being crucified for us to root out the ban blocking our return that had been so firmly fixed in place?[75]

Moreover, the mediating work of Christ, which offers a way to reorder love, is repeated in the ministry of the church through which the *uti/frui* distinction is made active not as the mere Platonic renunciation of the material, but as the reordering of love in the forgiveness of sins.[76] What this accomplishes first of all is a dramatic reimagining of simply everything (cosmology, politics, and so forth) in eschatological terms in such a way that moral change is the result:

75. Ibid., 1.17.16.
76. Ibid., 1.16.15; 1.18.17.

> Now indeed, the Lord's resurrection from the dead
> and his ascension into heaven, once believed, sup-
> ports our faith with a very great hope . . . Since, on
> the other hand, his coming is awaited from heaven
> as judge of the living and the dead, it strikes real fear
> in the hearts of the careless, to prompt their conver-
> sion to a more diligent practice of faith, so that by
> living good lives they may be in a position to desire
> his coming, rather than to dread it because they are
> living bad ones.[77]

The reordering of love is struck first in these terms, and it is
under these biblically dramatic terms that the rest of the discussion of *uti*-love and *frui*-love proceeds in book one.

That the ordering of love is essentially a form of *imitatio
Christi* is further displayed in the way Matthew 22 is used in
shaping the rest of book one. Anchoring the "great question,"
for Augustine, is Jesus's use of the *Shema*:

> This, after all, is the rule of love that God has set for
> us: *You shall love*, he says, *your neighbor as yourself; God*,
> however, *with your whole heart and your whole soul and
> your whole mind* . . . So all who love their neighbors in
> the right way ought so to deal with them that they too
> love with all their heart, all their soul, all their mind.
> By loving them, you see, in this way as themselves,
> they are relating all their love of themselves and of oth-
> ers to that love of God, which allows no channel to be
> led off from itself that will diminish its flow.[78]

What follows is an exploration into how one can love that
which is above and that which is equal to a lover—Augustine
assuming that the impulse to love the self is evident and that

77. Ibid., 1.15.14.
78. Ibid., 1.22.20–21.

loving what is beneath is an issue better treated indirectly.[79] In the reasoning that issues from this use of Matthew 22 is a basic recognition of the other person as like oneself, thinking of oneself "as the whole of you, that is your spirit and body, and your neighbor as the whole of him, namely his spirit and body." Even more, what is recognized in light of the rule of love here biblically presented is that love of the other person is of greater importance than the love of one's own body. This is the character of true love of self[80] in that it properly imitates Christ insofar as it uses the material (in sacrificing the body) correctly for the sake of the love of souls, which are loved insofar as God is loved first. This is the ordinate lover:

> But living a just and holy life requires one to be capable of an objective and impartial evaluation of things; to love things, that is to say, in the right order, so that you do not love what is not to be loved, or fail to love what is to be loved . . . And if God is to be loved more than any human being, we all ought to love God more than ourselves. Again, other people are to be loved more than our own bodies, because all these things are to be loved for God's sake, and other people are capable of enjoying God together with us, which our bodies cannot do, because what gives life to our bodies is our souls, and it is with these that we enjoy God.[81]

Again, despite the sometimes overemphasized Platonic division of body and soul, what more thoroughly determines Augustine's ordering of love is Jesus Christ, "Truth itself," who came in the flesh to be the mediator through whom believers are to come, at whom they are to arrive, and in whom they are to remain—a

79. Ibid., 1.23.22–23.
80. Ibid., 1.26.27.
81. Ibid., 1.27.28.

respite that is also with the Father.[82] This economy, so to speak, is basically a scriptural experience:

> So what all that has been said amounts to, while we have been dealing with things, is that the fulfillment and the end of the law and of all the divine scriptures is love; love of the thing which is to be enjoyed, and of the thing which is able to enjoy that thing together with us . . . So in order that we might know how to do this and be able to, the whole ordering of time was arranged by divine providence for our salvation.[83]

For Augustine, the christological ordering of love is shown forth in Scripture and is enacted in scriptural experience. Thus, what follows in the rest of *De Doctrina Christiana* is the service of that need for an appropriate scriptural experience—an experience of true biblical discipleship. All of this, the reordering of loves and knowledges, in turn, facilitates the ascent upon the sapiental ladder described in the second book, an ascent that brings the Christian into the moment of suffering theological redescription, the moment, potentially, of the martyr's re-narration of things in death:

> On fixing your gaze, to the extent that you are able, on this light as it sheds its rays from afar, and on perceiving that with your weak sight you cannot bear its brightness, you come to the fifth stage, that is to the stage of counsel which goes with mercy, and you purge your restless and ill-behaved soul of its appetite for inferior things and the dirt it has picked up from them. Here though, you drill yourself diligently in love of your neighbor, and come to perfection in it; and filled now with hope and having all your powers unimpaired, you climb up to the sixth stage, at which

82. Ibid., 1.34.38.
83. Ibid., 1.35.39.

you purge and clean those eyes with which God can
be seen, insofar as he can be by those who die to this
world, insofar as they can; because we see, to the extent that we do die to this world, while to the extent
that we live in this world, we do not see.[84]

What Augustine makes possible in his reordering of loves and
knowledges is none other than a theological "out-narration" of
Asad's notion of passive agency that begins to free the sort of
dying constitutive of Christian martyrdom from Perkins's ideological categories. This is, of course, a Milbankian reading of
Augustine, seeing *De Doctrina Christiana* as essentially a begin-
ner's guide to "metanarrative realism." Augustine here is filling
out a narrative that "interprets and 'locates' all other history."[85]
Moreover, certainly to Milbank's approval, Augustine here is
properly complex, showing that the metanarrative of Israel,
Jesus, and the Bible is also an ecclesiology that outlasts all social
sciences.[86] Regarding pain, Asad's argument that experiences
of pain are themselves modes of relationship is affirmed, but
Augustine in addition points to the person of the relationship
in the experience of Christian pain. Likewise, affirming both
Asad's and Perkins' argument that experiences of pain and their
representations are discursively mediated, Augustine unfolds a
hermeneutic habit that ensures a constantly renegotiated discursive experience that accepts all knowledges and all loves,
arbitrating them according to the christological love of God
and neighbor. Quite simply, what Augustine shows is that abso-
lutely everything, life and love and even death, is referenced, so
to speak, by the story told by Israel and the church.

84. Ibid., 2.7.11.

85. Milbank, *Theology and Social Theory*, 246. See also Wells, *Improvisa-tion*, 133.

86. Ibid., 385–87.

But what does this have to do with the role of death in Christian martyrdoms? That any discussion of subjectivity must issue from christological positioning within the story of Israel, Jesus, and the Church is clear from Augustine. The Church is the present moment of the story, so to speak. Yet why is suffering and sometimes death constitutive of Christian life and martyrdom? Does it do to simply point to Jesus's suffering and death as exemplary? Is Christian death sheer willful imitation of Christ's death, or is it also participation in his death as well? How is death read by Christians?

Maximus the Confessor's great contribution, perhaps more than any other late patristic theologian, was to take Chalcedon seriously. And in doing so he had to devote a great amount of his theological effort to what it means for a Christian to gaze upon and follow the dyothelitic Christ. Building on Cappadocian theological psychology and perhaps even some Augustinian influence,[87] Maximus traced out a soteriological ascesis that could imagine a "good use" for death—no longer in general Greek terms of escaping the body—but a "good use" for death that entailed the destruction of sin, the law of pleasure and pain, and eventually death itself.

For Maximus, God created humans with a spiritual capacity for enjoying God. Yet instantaneously, this capacity was spoiled in mistaking God for something material. This mistaken sensory pleasure was, therefore, affixed by God with pain "as a kind of punitive faculty, whereby the law of death was wisely implanted in our corporeal nature to curb the foolish mind in its desire

---

87. Berthold, "Did Maximus the Confessor Know Augustine?" 14–17 at 15. Berthold sees similarities particularly in their approaches to history and human freedom. Gregory of Nyssa is responsible for the notion of using the passions in Maximus (*Ad Thalassium* 1.47), yet in the *Chapters on Love* (2.17), for example, where he discusses the proper use of sexual intercourse, his teaching resembles Augustine's.

to incline unnaturally toward sensible things." The dialectic of pleasure and pain, for Maximus, was a sort of pedagogical rule whereby "the grace of the divine pleasure is exalted."[88] That is, in the life of pleasure and pain, the immaterial is preferred to the material.[89] Likewise this rule is just, as with its legacy, which arbitrates the whole of humanity. After the first transgression of natural pleasure, all "were tyrannized by unrighteous pleasure and naturally subject to just sufferings and to the thoroughly just death accompanying them."[90] According to Maximus, this dialectic of pleasure and pain is basic to fallen human nature. The only way that such a dialectic could be righted was "for an unjust and likewise uncaused suffering and death to be conceived—a death 'unjust' in the sense that it by no means followed a life given to passions, 'uncaused' in the sense that it was in no way preceded by pleasure." This unjust suffering and death was assumed by Jesus. His death was unjust because Jesus was the unique exception to the tyrannical dialectic of pain and pleasure. Unlike every other human, Jesus was born of a virgin, free from the usual "unrighteous pleasure" involved with procreation. Moreover, Jesus lived an ascetic life free from the constant tragedies of sensual pleasure. Because of this, Jesus's death was unjust in that it occurred without its usual provocation.

For Maximus, this is the mysterious moment of divine justice and the reordering of death. In breaking the cycle of pleasure and pain by keeping from unrighteous pleasure, Jesus invalidated the prerogatives of death. Jesus, fully divine and also fully human, "being composed just like us of an intellectual soul and a passible body, save only without sin," submitted to

88. *Ad Thalassium* 61.85.

89. This is a similar conclusion to that found in *Phaedo* 83b–c although the argument is different.

90. Ibid., 61.87.

the "condemnation imposed on our passibility and turned that very passibility into an instrument for eradicating sin and the death which is its consequence—or in other words for eradicating pleasure and the pain which is its consequence."[91] Breaking the causality of death in resisting the temptation of material pleasure, Jesus makes death an instrument:

> For death, once it has ceased having pleasure as its "birth-mother"—that pleasure for which death itself became the natural punishment—clearly becomes the "father" of everlasting life. Indeed, just as Adam's life of pleasure became the mother of death and corruption, so too our Lord's death for Adam's sake, being free of the pleasure inherited from Adam, became the father of eternal life.[92]

This is the inauguration of a new time, a time no longer for the destruction of human nature but for the destruction of sin. Human nature in Jesus resists the judgment of death and, so to speak, outlasts it. Because he does not suffer due to sin, but willingly, Jesus condemns sin in his suffering, making use of death and inviting others to make use of it as well:

> Because of Adam, who by his disobedience gave rise both to the law of birth through pleasure and the death of our nature which was its condemnation, all of his posterity who come into existence according to this law of birth through pleasure are necessarily subject—even if unwilling—to the death that is functionally linked with this birth and serves to condemn our nature. It was *time* for human nature to be condemned for its sin, while the law of birth through pleasure was ruling our nature. By contrast, because of Christ, who completely divested his human nature

91. Ibid., 61.89.
92. Ibid., 61.93.

of the law of birth through pleasure, and who willingly took up the use of death—which on Adam's account had condemned human nature—solely for purposes of condemning sin, all who in the Spirit are willingly reborn of Christ *with the bath of regeneration* are able by grace to put off their original Adamic birth based on pleasure.[93]

For Maximus, the prerogatives of death are changed by Jesus's death and resurrection. No longer is death read as corruption or escape; rather, in Christ, and in those adopted through baptism, death becomes the very site of peace and deification. For the adopted, death marks not simply the stark terms of an irreconcilable conflict (as with Perkins), nor is it merely relational (as with Asad); for the baptized, death is itself useful as the moment of peace and as the moment of union and glorification, leading eventually to "divine and unending life."[94]

What Maximus's theological reading of death exemplifies is just what Augustine was doing in *De Doctrina Christiana*. It is not right to suggest that Maximus was laying down theories of theodicy and atonement. What Maximus was doing was reading the world through the dyothelitic Christ. That is, in discovering Christ scripturally and creedally Maximus found a way to re-narrate life and death as love and peace. Death becomes sacrifice because it participates in the beauty of refusing the sensual and violent economy of sin. Perhaps this explains something of the alleged pathology of some of the early Christian martyrs. Ignatius desired to be ground like wheat in the teeth of the beasts not out of some death wish; rather, in being ground like eucharistic bread Ignatius was making the amphitheater another Calvary. His death was not just imitation; it was a participation in the peaceful pleading of Jesus's death before the

93. Ibid., 61.97.
94. Ibid., 61.99.

Father. Potentially every death is converted by Christ's death. Blandina's death not only resembled Christ's crucifixion, it shared in it. Blandina was sacrificed because in the performance of her death she extended the nonviolence of Christ's obedience to the Father. Suffering and death, just as the good confession, is constitutive of martyrdom because the Christian who suffers has no other means to realize the sovereignty of God than to confess Jesus as Lord. This is simply another way of talking about resurrection. The resurrection does not erase death or correct the balance. The resurrection characterizes death as peace. Death is used. It is without its sting and victory.

MARTYRDOM AS OVERACCEPTANCE

In reading the confession of the early martyrs in Barthian terms of the peaceable vocation of witness, and in reading their deaths in terms of performing that vocation in the refusal of violence, it then becomes possible to describe the moment of martyrdom succinctly by employing Samuel Wells's notion of overacceptance.

Following Milbank's theology of ontological peace, Wells further deconstructs ethics built upon logics of scarcity and death. Wells questions the "givens" of any ethics that rely on arguments from a realism that enshrines the apriority of certain ideas regarding human or social nature, economics, or metaphysics. These givens, according to Wells, predetermine the scope of imagination and action within a story not all together clear but still dominant. For Wells, the only given in Christian ethics is "God's story, the theo-drama, the church's narrative."[95] Everything else is always potentially a gift. That is, no event or determination or maneuver can possibly bring an end to the

95. Wells, *Improvisation*, 125.

story in which Christians read themselves. Even evil, along with anything good or apparently good, cannot finally determine the story of Israel and the church. The church's theological task, then, is not a matter of preserving some pristine account of the good or sacred. Rather, the ethical task of the church is being skillful and creative enough to continue to read its own story in a way that encodes the whole history of the world with the hope the church performs in its liturgy and friendships. This is what Wells means by overacceptance. It is a skill in receiving the mundane "without losing the initiative."[96] It is a way of taking a particular moment and locating it within a larger story in such a way that that moment is now read within the larger narrative. That is, the church is a people who are always able to move the story forward:

> They are able to say "And . . . ?" to their oppressors because they know that their own deaths do not mark the end of God's story. When the church is able to face the threats of the world with the same "And . . . ?" it gains extraordinary moral power. This is a power far greater than any physical power it might sometimes have assumed it needed. The courage to accept in this way is derived from its Lord. For the power of Christ lies in the fact that he accepted death, even death on a cross; he was able to do so because he believed in the "And." He believed that his death was not the end of the story: and so it proved. When the church says "And . . . ?" it is faithfully imitating Christ. It is in this faithful imitation that the church finds the power to confront the threats of the world without being intimidated.[97]

96. Ibid., 131.
97. Ibid., 110.

The skill of overacceptance is precisely that which is exemplified in Augustine, Maximus, and even Barth. In *De Doctrina Christiana* Augustine overaccepted the loves and knowledges of the pagan world saying, "all good and true Christians should understand that truth, wherever they may find it, belongs to their Lord."[98] When Maximus called death the father of life, he was encoding death with the resurrection thereby making death a time for peace. When Barth, describing Christian existence in terms of the peaceable vocation of witness, says, "Basically and finally all things will work together for good to him in both time and eternity . . . His regard must be first for the kingdom . . . what is right in the light of its coming,"[99] he was overaccepting the egotistical conventions of European Christianity. Likewise, in the amphitheater when Sanctus replied in Latin, "I am a Christian," he overaccepted every other identification possible with their usual violence. In describing overacceptance, Wells illumines something basic to theology and Christian practice. He describes a theological style, which destabilizes the tradition of theological positions. Overaccepting is fundamentally a liturgical and biblical skill. It is a way of reading the story of Israel and the church in every possible place.

Another way to speak of overacceptance is to speak of peace and patience. John Howard Yoder summarizes all of the above in terms of peace that is reminiscent of Maximus's use of death and in terms of patience more patient than Barth. For Yoder, commitments to peace without eschatology are unintelligible in that they describe peace in terms not defined by the Christian story. Peace, for Yoder, names "a hope, which defying present frustration, defines a present position in terms of the yet

98. Augustine *Teaching Christianity* 2.18.28.

99. Barth, *Church Dogmatics* IV/3.2, 593.

unseen goal which gives it meaning."[100] The goal is that which is continuously rehearsed by Israel and the church:

> The ultimate meaning of history is to be found in the work of the church . . . The victory of the Lamb through his death seals the victory of the church. Her suffering, like her Master's, is the measure of her obedience to the self-giving love of God. Nonresistance is right, in the deepest sense, not because it works, but because it anticipates the triumph of the Lamb that was slain.[101]

The Church exemplifies the way God deals with evil by imitating the way he dealt with evil in Jesus—by refusing the security won by violence and without God. Like Maximus, Yoder sees Christian life as sharing in a new time, a time that converts evil and death. For Yoder, it is characteristic of Christ and the Church "that evil, without being blotted out is channelized by God, in spite of itself, to serve His purposes."[102] Thus, for Christians, their commitments to peace in imitation of Jesus require patience stronger than death. The cross sets the limits of Christian patience.

Overacceptance in peace and patience is also precisely what early Christian martyrs were doing in saying, "I am a Christian." Also by enduring torture and death, as the author of the Lyons account reports, they were making "light of their great burden as they sped on to Christ, proving without question *that the sufferings of the present time are not to be compared with the glory that shall be revealed in us.*"[103] These were not, to be fair, ideological zealots. In witnessing to the sovereignty of Jesus

---

100. Yoder, *Original Revolution*, 53.

101. Ibid., 61.

102. Ibid., 59.

103. *Martyrs of Lyons* 1.6.

and in embracing the nonviolence implicit in that claim, early Christian martyrs were not seeking to destroy the Roman *mos maiorum* as much as they were trying to reorder it within the promise made to Abraham. That is, the martyrs' conflicts were not civilization clashes only; they were also radical moments of evangelism. It was perhaps only later, after Constantine, that the martyrs could have ever been thought to be pioneers of a Christian civilization.

CHAPTER 3

𝕻ilgrim 𝕳oliness

THE JUDGMENTS OF MARTYRDOM

> "Christianity is not a doctrine, not, I mean, a theory
> about what has happened and will happen to
> the human soul, but a description of something
> *that actually takes place in human life.*"
>
> —Ludwig Wittgenstein, *Culture and Value*, 28

ATTALUS'S ANTANACLASIS

Attalus was carried around the arena behind a sign that read, "This is Attalus, the Christian." He would have been killed then, after rousing up the mob, had not the governor learned of his Roman citizenship and sent him back to prison to await the emperor's decision.[1] Meanwhile, as the account continues, Alexander the Phrygian was arrested for being a Christian. Alexander was a physician and a teacher, "known practically to everyone because of his love of God and his outspokenness in preaching the word." Together, on the following day these two were tortured and killed. Alexander, the physician preacher,

---

1. *Martyrs of Lyons* 1.43–44.

"uttered no groan or any cry at all, but simply spoke to God in his heart." Attalus died differently. The account gives a sense of quickened frustration and chaos surrounding Attalus's end, as the mob again demanded his torture and death, bypassing the benefits of his citizenship, which should have afforded him a quick beheading. In the rush Attalus was submitted to the tortures of the arena. He was attached to the "brazen seat," and while burning he cried out to the spectators of his own death: "Look you, what you are doing is cannibalism! We Christians are not cannibals, nor do we perform any other sinful act."[2] Offering up, out from under the bondage of his own death, as both the flames and the eyes of the spectators consumed his flesh, Attalus spoke. His words described the scene; they were guilty of cannibalism, not the Christians. In his death Attalus reversed the dominant narrative of Lyons. In giving up his body to be consumed, he was able to reveal the hidden triumph that constitutes the hope of the confession, the *magnificat* reversal of the powerful and powerless, rich and poor. From Attalus's words, there broke open a whole new world.

Attalus's reversal is by no means unique in the martyr accounts. Time and again there are exchanges between accuser and accused, condemned and onlooker, which display a type of *antanaclasis*, a sort of rhetorical reversal of meaning that reveals in a moment an alternative description of the scene. For example, Polycarp, having been brought into the amphitheater, was implored by the governor, "Have respect for your age . . . Recant. Say, 'Away with the atheists!'" In sober response Polycarp looked up to heaven and then glanced at the mob of the arena, shook his fist at them and said, "Away with the atheists!"[3] In an instant, as if stealing the words of his accusers, Polycarp described the

2. Ibid., 1.52.

3. *Martyrdom of St. Polycarp* 9.2.

scene differently, reversing the very representations of the language of power.

What is going on in these moments of rhetorical reversal? Were these martyrs simply quick witted? Are they tricksters in the way that Scott and Boyarin describe Brer Rabbit[4] and Rabbi Eli'ezer?[5] Or are these martyr acts simply texts in which such exchanges provide elements of entertainment? Repeatedly, throughout the martyr acts, scenes of conventional power and domination, suffering and death are turned upside down, revealing not what is an illusory inversion of reality according to the dominant narrative of power but what is, according to the narrative that the martyrs embody, a fresh disclosure of a new reality.

The purpose of this final chapter is to explore these moments of reversal. When the proconsul asked Pionius, "Why do you rush towards death?" what was it for the martyr to answer, "I'm not rushing towards death . . . but towards life"?[6] Was this bold false consciousness? Or was this the community's way of salvaging the defeat of their fallen heroes? It is the suggestion of this chapter that something deeper is going on. After exploring the totalizing tendencies in some philosophy and theology, looking especially at Hegel, a tenderer philosophical explication of just what the martyrs were doing will be argued from a reading of Wittgenstein. In reading Wittgenstein and the martyr acts together it will be possible to suggest that the martyrs exemplify what it is to be truthful as far as Christians can be. That is, it will be possible to see how martyrs describe the world, turning it upside down with a peaceable and vulnerable discourse, with words that escape even their own control. In the martyrs it is possible to see what it means to speak in the present moment,

4. Scott, *Domination*, 163.

5. Boyarin, *Dying for God*, 27.

6. *Martyrdom of Pionius the Presbyter* 20.5

in truth and the Spirit.[7] Likewise, in their speech it is possible to learn something about forgiveness.

BREAKING HEGEL'S CIRCLE

Hegel belongs in a discussion on the descriptive capacity of early martyrs' speech because he is really the first significant thinker of the modern period most concerned with the philosophical commitments and import of historical contingencies. Reacting to both an arid Enlightenment rationalism erected in abstraction as well as the more irrational flights of fancy exhibited in the Romantics, Hegel attempted to behold the total system while at the same time respecting the particularity of history.[8] Surveying what he perceived to be the whole of history, he thought it "this process of development and the realization of spirit—this is true *Theodicæa*, the justification of God in history."[9] Epic though it was, his is a project that ultimately fails; nonetheless Hegel, perhaps unlike Kant, would at least have taken the martyrs seriously on a philosophical level.

Hegel's project is meant to be overwhelming. Terms are meant to collapse into oblivion, and philosophical innovation is meant to be unsettling and restless until the Absolute comes to be from out of its virtual occlusion. Following Hegel's own way of putting it, being is the movement of consciousness. Consciousness arises naturally yet mysteriously as "immediate consciousness,"[10] emerging as simply direct awareness of itself. When the self begins to reflect upon its own consciousness, as "*cultivated* consciousness," consciousness discovers, or more

---

7. Mark 13:11.

8. West, *An Introduction to Continental Philosophy*, 35.

9. Hegel, *Philosophy of History*, 457.

10. Hegel, *Phenomenology of Spirit*, sec. 789, 480.

specifically, traduces something beyond itself, "the Thing."[11] Here develops "*moral self-consciousness*," an awareness of "*essence*," something at once alien and itself.[12] All of this is reconciled as Spirit, showing the Spirit to have been primordially virtual ("*in principle*"[13]) and then actual:

> This first movement changes round into the second, since this element of recognition posits itself, as *simple* knowledge of duty, in antithesis to the *distinction* and *dichotomy* that lie in action as such and so constitute a stubborn actuality confronting action. But in forgiveness, we saw how this obstinacy surrenders and renounces itself. Here, therefore, actuality as well as *immediate existence* has for self-consciousness no other significance than that of being a pure knowing, similarly, as *determinate* existence or as relation, what is self-opposed is a knowing, partly of this individual Self, partly of knowledge as universal. In this is posited at the same time that the *third* movement, the *universality* or *essence*, counts only as *knowledge* for each of the two sides that stand over against each other; and finally these latter equally resolve the empty antithesis still remaining and are the knowledge of 'I'='I'; this *individual* Self which is immediately a pure knowing or a universal.[14]

Yet this pure knowledge is not lost in some sort of Kantian ether. Hegel's project attempts to behold totality while at the same time preserving some ontological status for contingency, investing the heritage of consciousness with the "true Notion," which is "the knowing of pure knowledge, not as an abstract

---

11. Ibid., sec. 791, 481; italics here and in subsequent quotes are in original.

12. Ibid., sec. 792, 481.

13. Ibid., sec. 795, 483.

14. Ibid., sec. 793, 482.

essence such as duty is, but of knowledge as an essential being which is *this* knowledge, *this* pure self-consciousness which is, therefore, at the same time a genuine *object*, for the Notion is the Self that is for itself."[15] The image Hegel employs here is a circle:

> The movement is the circle that returns into itself, the circle that presupposes its beginning and reaches it only at the end. Hence, so far as Spirit is necessarily this immanent differentiation, its intuited whole appears over against its simple self-consciousness, and since, then, the former is what is differentiated, it is differentiated into its intuited pure Notion, into *Time* and into the content or into the *in-itself*.[16]

The circle displays for Hegel both the virtual priority of Spirit as well as the ontic legacy of contingency. It is at this moment that Hegel begins to develop a philosophy of history. Giving depth to the circle, Hegel at once temporalizes metaphysics and eternalizes history, for although Spirit develops upon the circle, "it is none the less on a higher level than it starts." Thus, the "realm of Spirits which is formed in this way in the outer world constitutes a succession in Time in which one Spirit relieved another of its charge and each took over the empire of the world from its predecessor."[17] Here, at the evolutionary pinnacle of Hegel's project, metaphysics transposes history, and the chroniclers give way to the historians.

This movement, as well, is by no means the sleek abstraction of contemplation. Rather, there is at the heart of Hegel's movement of consciousness the necessity of contingency, of

15. Ibid., sec., 795, 484.
16. Ibid., sec. 802, 488.
17. Ibid., sec. 808, 492.

passions, and what John Burbidge translates as "abrasion."[18] Dialectic, for Hegel, is rough business, of reason making the best of the irrational, the one-off, disaster, and charisma:

> Over and over again he stresses the critical role of the negative—of that which contradicts, challenges, disrupts and destroys. Reason works with cunning, for it not only brings about something universal, but it does so by allowing the particular and idiosyncratic to have free play. And whenever the particular stakes its claim, the overarching generality of the universal is put in question. So reason requires and uses the irrationality of the passions. What is rational emerges as the way this irrationality has found of producing a comprehensive picture, an achievement which is itself destined to be disrupted once again by reactions of passionate force.[19]

As with his metaphysical system broadly, so too with his version of dialectic, Hegel attempts to find a place for the odd, the evil, and the unexpected within a totality. His is a theodicy project ultimately, one that seeks some consolation of redemption for contingency. It is a project that sought to preserve the historical for the respect of the eternal. As Hegel himself presented it, it was a short-lived project although tremendously influential in its derivations. Yet philosophically, the deepest irony of Hegel's project is that although it attempts to preserve the ontic legacy of contingency within history, it actually occludes the historical, giving ground to many lesser ideologies through history as well as annihilating contingency within a necessary totality.

Such was the critique of Johannes Climacus, Kierkegaard's pseudonym. For him it was impossible to articulate an existential system; the notion was a ridiculous contradiction. "Existence

18. Burbidge, *Hegel's Systematic Contingency*, 5.

19. Ibid., 7.

itself is a system," Climacus would allow, but only for God; "it cannot be a system for any existing spirit."[20] It was the very idea of a system, which, for Climacus, meant closure and finality that was itself the closure and finality of the constitutive volatility of existence. Hegel could not have both system and existence without pantheism,[21] creating a sort of double illusion of both totality and existence. "The systematic idea is subject-object, is the unity of thinking and being." [22] Existence, though, resists such identification. To gather existence and finality into a single philosophical glance was to sacrifice the existent to an idol of totality; existence as a concept "fantastically volatilizes."[23] Climacus correctly perceived that such a project was antithetical to proper Christian notions of subjectivity:

> Christianity, therefore, protests against all objectivity; it wants the subject to be infinitely concerned about himself. What it asks about is the subjectivity; the truth of Christianity, if it is at all, is only in this; objectively, it is not at all. And even if it is only in one single subject, then it is only in him, and there is greater Christian joy in heaven over this one than over world history and the system, which as objective powers are incommensurate with the essentially Christian.[24]

What Climacus understood was that contingency, especially the contingency basic to Christianity, could not remain freely

---

20. Kierkegaard, *Concluding Unscientific Postscript*, 118. I am not going to undertake the exegesis necessary to clarify issues arising from the psuedonymity of Johannes Climacus. On this, see Hartshorne, *Kierkegaard, Godly Deceiver*.

21. Or, more precisely, panentheism. See Fox, *Accessible Hegel*, 95.

22 Kierkegaard, *Concluding Unscientific Postscript*, 123.

23. Ibid., 122.

24. Ibid., 130.

and genuinely contingent within the necessity of a metaphysical system.

This critique probes the weakness of Hegel's project directly. The tragedy of Hegel's metaphysical project is twofold, being both illusory and violent. The problem with the image of the circle is that although it gives the illusion of totality, with each successive development of consciousness recapitulating every previous moment, the suggestion of infinity is itself at best chimerical. And although Hegel attempts to provide some depth to the circle, giving a sense of history, it is only a mirage. The circle suggests completion when such comprehension is impossible within the world of contingent beings. It is an idol, for what could ever suggest that the circle is indeed complete? It can only be put forward in silence. Moreover, as the sinister history of modernity displays, such a totalizing view can only be secured by force. And that such a project tends toward totalitarianism is by no means surprising either. For after the state has been fundamentally involved within metaphysics as history, and following Marx's politicization of Hegel, once this was given over to the "vulgarity of mob leaders," the state became the violent and totalizing servant of national mythologies.[25] As David Bentley Hart points out, in Hegel's system when "violence—indeed, warfare—is imagined as inextricable from being," then being "proves itself uninhabitable . . . and becomes all too transparently an abstract violence enacted against the concrete innocence of becoming, the canopy of the 'Same' cast over the extravagant openness of difference (or a cloud floating above an abyss)."[26] Thus, what results from Hegel's project is perhaps the most compelling metaphysical idol of modernity.

---

25. Arendt, *Origins of Totalitarianism*, 249. The relation between Hegel's historicism and totalitarianism is argued explicitly by Karl Popper. See his *Open Society*, 2:27–80.

26. Hart, *Beauty of the Infinite*, 38.

In its attempt to preserve history for philosophy, Hegel's circle only succeeds in destroying it. The circle seduces those who behold it into shifting their gaze away from the historical toward an illusive and ultimately totalitarian wholeness.

Such is the philosophical idolatry that corrupts any genuine grasp of early martyrs' speech. Given the totalitarian legacy of trying to perceive the whole, reading the sometimes cryptic eschatological statements of the martyrs, or their sometimes colorful or bizarre exchanges with either persecutors or the mobs, can be construed unduly as a sort of gnostic arrogance. That is, given modern systematic pretense, such martyrs' speech can be misread as attempts to supply their own totalities to the chaos of their defeat and death. For example, in *The Martyrdom of Saints Perpetua and Felicitas*, to those who had come to watch the condemned eat their last meal, Saturus, a Christian, said, "Will not tomorrow be enough for you? Why are you so eager to see something that you dislike? Our friends today will be our enemies on the morrow. But take careful note of what we look like so that you will recognize us on the day."[27] This is inevitably read as totalizing bravado, as an arrogance issuing from some secret perception of the whole. Thus, as with Perkins's and Young's misunderstanding of the martyrs as embodying an irreconcilable and total clash with a late antique religious system, here again the martyrs' speech is misconstrued. Such speech can be problematically read as violent and intransigent, as speech that is itself a mere sigh of power issuing from a holistic false consciousness.

Early martyrs' speech is certainly not this. Rather, as will be argued below, whenever the martyrs spoke in refracted meaning, or eschatologically, or cryptically, what they exemplified was a mode of truthfulness nearer to what could be described

27. *Martyrdom of Saints Perpetua and Felicitas* 17.2.

as *pilgrim holiness*. That is, their speech was offered much more humbly and occasionally, under constraint, and with a sort of gasping hope. The martyrs saw just what their persecutors saw, yet they spoke differently—from hope.

BETTER WITTGENSTEINIANS

As much as Hegel, Wittgenstein belongs in a conversation about the capacity of early martyrs' speech too. Wittgenstein's refusal of epistemological categories disposes him to listen to the martyrs' seemingly erratic speech more clearly than perhaps any other philosopher. One would think that Wittgenstein would have been fascinated by the martyr accounts, and it would have been equally fascinating to discover what he would have made of these stories. Yet without any such aphorisms on the martyrs, it is possible to suggest that Wittgenstein offers something for reflection here by his sense of what could be described as the mystical aspect, or better, the mystical pregnancy of language. Simply, it is the argument of this section that Wittgenstein allows the martyrs to be heard more freely; and not only that, in return, the martyrs actually prove better Wittgensteinians than Wittgenstein.

Deploying Wittgenstein against the metaphysical projects of the likes of Hegel is nothing remarkable. Risking some crudity, one of Wittgenstein's favorite sayings succinctly diagnoses Hegel's mistake: "You cannot shit higher than your arse."[28] As with Kierkegaard and others, through Wittgenstein, Hegel's metaphysical bravado is made apparent. What Wittgenstein exemplifies in contrast is not just a humbler way of risking knowledge, he makes it possible finally to attend to the narrative imagination of the martyrs themselves. In particular, in *On Certainty*, Wittgenstein suggests a way in which martyrs' speech

28. Quoted in Blackburn, *Truth*, 57.

could be understood as an example of changing language games, of describing the world anew.

In *On Certainty*, Wittgenstein is trying to show how rationality as representation, or more specifically how any rendition of a correspondence theory of truth, cannot constitute a transcendental epistemology that removes a person from the burden of language. What Wittgenstein is trying to show is a way of knowing that, contrary to Moore's desire for more solid ground, is content to be rooted in present language alone, without the desire of constructing another conceptual justification for what is present in the language in use. For example, in aphorisms 508 through 511:

508. What can I rely on?

509. I really want to say that a language-game is only possible if one trusts something (I did not say "can trust something").

510. If I can say "Of course I know that that's a towel" I am making an utterance. I have not thought of verification. For me it is an immediate utterance.

   I don't think of past or future. (And of course it's the same for Moore, too.)

   It is just like directly taking hold of something, as I take hold of my towel without having doubts.

511. And yet this direct taking-hold corresponds to a sureness, not to a knowing.

   But don't I take hold of a thing's name like that, too?[29]

Within a language game there are elements of language that must be certain in order for there to be further judgments made that would themselves further constitute the language game as it moves on. These basic elements, "scaffolding" in the early

29. Wittgenstein, *On Certainty*, 508–11 (Paul and Anscombe, 66e–67e).

language of the *Tractatus*,[30] must serve as empirical propositions within the language game even if there is no transcendental way to know, or more precisely to speak, of their empirical status. For example, in aphorism 308:

> 308. "Knowledge" and "certainty" belong to different *categories*. They are not two "mental states" like, say "surmising" and "being sure" . . . What interests us now is not being sure but knowledge. That is, we are interested in the fact that about certain empirical propositions no doubt can exist if making judgments is to be possible at all. Or again: I am inclined to believe that not everything that has the form of an empirical proposition *is* one.[31]

Judgments are those further moments of a language game that follow upon more basic elements of the game acknowledged as beyond doubt[32] and which make for the intelligible action of any person within a language game. For example, in aphorisms 196 through 200:

> 196. Sure evidence is what we *accept* as sure, it is evidence that we go by in *acting* surely, acting without any doubt.
>
>   What we call "a mistake" plays a quite special part in our language games, and so too does what we regard as certain evidence.
>
> 197. It would be nonsense to say that we regard something as sure evidence because it is certainly true.
>
> 198. Rather, we must first determine the role of deciding for or against a proposition.
>
> 199. The reason why the use of the expression "true or false" has something misleading about it is that it

---

30. Wittgenstein, *Wittgenstein's Tractatus*, 6.124 (Kolak, 42).
31. Wittgenstein, *On Certainty*, 308 (Paul and Anscombe, 39e).
32. Ibid., 378 (49e).

> is like saying "it tallies with the facts or it doesn't",
> and the very thing that is in question is what "tal-
> lying" is here.
>
> 200. Really "The proposition is either true or false"
> only means that it must be possible to decide for
> or against it. But this does not say what the ground
> for such a decision is like.[33]

Basic elements of a language game serve a sort of inaugural and arbitrating logical role that facilitate all further judgments. As Wittgenstein asks, "Indeed, doesn't it seem obvious that the possibility of a language-game is conditioned by certain facts?"[34] And the world of such a language game is itself something un-burdened by the pretensions of transcendental certainty; it is, rather, a more persuasive world, which is by no means inoculated against violence, but a world of heretics, pagans, and salvation. It is a world in which sides must be taken and masters followed, the sort of world intimated in aphorisms 611 and 612:

> 611. Where two principles really do meet which cannot
> be reconciled with one another, then each man
> declares the other a fool and heretic.
>
> 612. I said I would "combat" the other man—but
> wouldn't I give him *reasons*? Certainly; but how far
> do they go? At the end of reasons comes *persuasion*.
> (Think what happens when missionaries convert
> natives.)[35]

This is a world of enlivened aesthetics, a world that is not only envisioned but enacted. It is a world in which invitation redeems argument, discipleship redeems pedagogy, and beauty displays truth. Again, it is a world suggested in aphorisms 204 and 206:

33. Ibid., 196–200 (27e).

34. Ibid., 617 (82e).

35. Ibid., 611–12 (81e).

204. Giving grounds, however, justifying the evidence, comes to an end;—but the end is not certain propositions' striking us immediately as true, i.e. it is not a kind of *seeing* on our part; it is our *acting*, which lies at the bottom of the language-game.

206. If someone asked us "but is that *true*?" we might say "yes" to him; and if he demanded grounds we might say "I can't give you any grounds, but if you learn more you too will think the same."

If this didn't come about, that would mean that he couldn't for example learn history.[36]

That is, following Wittgenstein, a language game is unpredictable, "It is there—like our life."[37] It is a world not of transcendental seeing and then acting, but of seeing and acting together.

At this juncture it becomes possible to think of the descriptive capacity of language and, in turn, martyrs' language. It is possible for language games to change and for language to describe the world anew: "When language-games change, then there is a change in concepts, and with the concepts the meanings of words change."[38] In the Lyons story there are fault lines present within the account itself, suggesting that these martyrdoms display, in Wittgenstein's terms, a change from one language game to another:

Thus the servants, ensnared by Satan and terrified of the tortures that saw the faithful suffering, at the soldiers' instigation falsely accused the Christians of Oedipean marriages and dinners in the manner of Thyestes, and many other things that it would be sinful for us even to think of or speak about—indeed, one doubts whether such things ever happened among men at all. But these stories got about and all

36. Ibid., 204, 206 (28e).
37. Ibid., 559 (73e).
38. Ibid., 65 (10e).

the people raged against us, so that even those whose attitude had been moderate before because of their friendship with us now became greatly angry and gnashed their teeth at us. Thus the Lord's saying was proved true: *The time is coming when whoever kills you will think he is doing service to God.*[39]

It is within this instability that Attalus was able to offer up his body to the spectacular cannibalism of the crowd, describing the world anew with the words, "Look you, what you are doing is cannibalism!"[40] Parsing these martyrdoms in a Wittgensteinian fashion, what is happening in these deaths are the judgments of a new language game. No longer are the *aprioris* beyond doubt the basic fixtures of the Roman *mos maiorum*; rather, among Christians they are simply that Jesus is Lord and not Caesar. As Speratus, one of Scillitan martyrs, responded,

I do not recognize the empire of this world. Rather, I serve the God whom no man has seen, nor can see, with these eyes. I have not stolen; and on any purchase I pay the tax, for I acknowledge my lord who is the emperor of kings and of all the nations.[41]

The meaning of "lord," "empire," and "king" changes in the martyrs' speech, and so, in turn, do the judgments regarding atheism, theft, cannibalism, suffering, and so on. When Polycarp says, "Away with the atheists!" the crowd has indeed newly become atheists.[42] The language game has changed.

But recalling earlier Hegelian concerns, what is the scope of this change? If it is not the arrogance of some totalizing bravado, then what is it? Here Wittgenstein refuses to offer any

---

39. *Martyrs of Lyons* 1.14–15.

40. Ibid., 1.52.

41. *Acts of the Scillitan Martyrs* 6.

42. *Martyrdom of St. Polycarp* 9.2.

comforting suggestion at all, offering, at best, silence. J. Mark Lazenby, in arguing an alternative reading of the *Tractatus*, insists that what Wittgenstein was trying to accomplish was not an analytical banishment of the mystical, but instead a reconstruction of the mystical within the analytical. That is, what began in the *Tractatus* and developed in later work was Wittgenstein's attempt to recover the unempirical pieces ("important nonsense") of language for a more meaningful factual discourse:

> Important nonsense undoes reliance on nonsense that detracts from living in the present. Important nonsense, like the passages in the *Tractatus*, which set out the limit of factual discourse, is nonetheless nonsense, and like unimportant nonsense, we must give it up. We cannot give it up, however, until we take it seriously, until, that is, we are able to live completely and without remainder in the present, the cardinal indication of which is that all we say is factual. (A test of whether some piece of nonsense is important nonsense is whether the nonsense spurs one to speak only in factual discourse. Unimportant nonsense invariably spurs one to say something metaphysical— garden variety gibberish.)[43]

Lazenby's interpretation of early Wittgenstein is important for this discussion for what it gets right and for what it gets wrong. Recalling the mystical pregnancy, so to speak, of factual discourse, as Lazenby does, it is easier to read early martyrs' speech as something not escapist, totalizing, arrogant, or ideological. That is, when the martyrs said that Jesus is Lord, and when they made succeeding judgments, they were indeed speaking to the present moment. However, what Lazenby gets wrong illustrates something about martyrs' speech as well. He makes the argument that Wittgenstein's notion of the mystical quality of

43. Lazenby, *Early Wittgenstein on Religion*, 78.

language turns on the "reconstructed meanings" of nonsensical words like "eternity" and "God." Lazenby argues that theology "must reconstruct the meanings of words that have lost the ability to keep us in the present. These new meanings, to break out of metaphysical nonsensicality, must describe what actually takes place in human life."[44] That is, for Lazenby, words like "God" and "eternity" must name realities of factual, immanent discourse; they must be redeemed from "garden variety gibberish." What is remarkable about this argument, and wrong, is that it repeats the mistake that Wittgenstein warned about, of thinking what cannot be thought. It is one thing to suggest that factual discourse is mystical and another thing to conclude that "God" cannot mean something beyond its use in factual discourse. How does Lazenby know this? Indeed, it seems that Lazenby's mistake highlights what is so powerful in martyrs' speech. For the utterances of the martyrs, the present world is not reconstructed but described, and thereby that world is intensified. Yet, their speech is not closed; rather, it is open to the later memory of the church and also the judgment of God. For the martyrs to say that Jesus is Lord was to speak explicitly in and to their present world, but it was also to speak in such a way as to open up themselves and the world to further nuances of factual discourse. This is what it means for the martyrs to speak eschatologically. To follow Lazenby's mistake would be to read again into the martyr stories the clash of ideologies and the removal of history. In leaving martyrs' speech open to judgment, while at the same time retaining Wittgenstein's and Lazenby's reminders about present, factual discourse, the martyrs become those who confess a whole new world for which God waits to reenter its history and show himself face to face.

44. Ibid., 80.

Before moving on from Wittgenstein to flesh out martyrs's speech as present description, a small and respectful *ad
hominem* argument will return the discussion from the likes
of Hegel and Wittgenstein back to the brutality of the arena:
When missionaries go into foreign lands, they talk about saving pagans. When Christians talk about their lives, they talk
about dying with Christ in baptism as they feel the waters sur-
round them, or feeding on him in the Eucharist as they taste
bread and wine; they talk about prayer with their knees, rosa-
ries with their hands, confession with their tears, and so on.
What they do not talk about are language games. The irony of
Wittgenstein's project is that it keeps such ordinary language
at bay, which is exactly what seems to be the problem. Thus,
if acting is what language games are about,[45] then the martyrs
are better Wittgensteinians than Wittgenstein. In the Lyons account, those who had survived their torture refused to be called
martyrs: "if anyone of us would speak of them as martyrs either
by word or letter, they would sharply rebuke him." For these
burned, bruised, and wounded Christians, only Jesus and those
who had actually died could be called martyrs:

> And they would recall the martyrs that had already
> passed away, saying: "They were indeed martyrs,
> whom Christ has deigned to take up in their hour of
> confession, putting his seal on their witness by death:
> but we are simple, humble confessors." With tears
> they begged their fellow Christians, asking that abun-
> dant prayers be offered that they might be perfected.
> Although they manifested the power of martyrdom
> in deed, speaking to the pagans with great openness,
> and showing forth their nobility by their persever-
> ance, fearlessness, and courage, none the less they
> begged that the name of martyr not be used of them

45. Wittgenstein, *On Certainty*, 204 (28e).

among the Christians, filled as they were with the fear of God.[46]

Death was the seal and perfection of the martyr's language game, at best analogous to Wittgenstein's silent final proposition in the *Tractatus*. For the confessors, having suffered just short of physical death, there was still room, that is, some distance, that remained between sharing completely in the witness of Jesus and their own confession. Ignatius of Antioch perhaps most vividly displays this distance and his longing to overcome it throughout his letters, such as when he begs the Romans not to interfere with his pending death, praying that he "may be given sufficient inward and outward strength to be as resolute in will as in words, and a Christian in reality instead of only in repute." For Ignatius, "the work we have to do is no affair of persuasive speaking; Christianity lies in achieving greatness in the face of a world's hatred."[47] Pionius desired to close the same distance, protesting to Polemon, the temple verger, "You have been ordered either to persuade us or to punish us. You are not persuading us. So, inflict the punishment."[48] For the martyrs, to use Wittgenstein's terms, Christ was the perfect actualization of the language game; thus, sharing in his life, death, and eventually his resurrection was the only condition in which Christians could inhabit the language game. There was simply no other way to give witness. To defer to some other language, which was to defer death, was to invite the suggestion that Jesus himself need not have died, or to imply that there were double language games possible. For Ignatius, martyrdom without death risked making everything an illusion: "After all, if everything the Lord did was an illusion, then these chains of mine must be illusory

46. *Martyrs of Lyons* 2.3–4.

47. Ignatius of Antioch *Letter to the Romans* 3.

48. *Martyrdom of Pionius the Presbyter* 8.1

too!"[49] For him, "the fine words of our so-called intellectuals" were insufficient.[50] Death was *the* story, not the exchangeable ornament of a story that could have had other features instead. For Ignatius and other martyrs, talk of language games would have been for those outside of the arena, or in Wittgenstein's case, for the liminal monastic gardener.[51] The distance closed in the martyrs remained uncrossed, sometimes despairingly and in the end awkwardly for Wittgenstein. Having once embraced Tolstoy's Christianity, Wittgenstein could never genuinely inhabit the Christian language game, which would have been to renounce language games for baptism, Eucharist, and discipleship. His funeral according to the Catholic rite was awkwardly done, and just before his death Wittgenstein wondered:

> God may say to me: "I am judging you out of your own mouth. Your actions have made you shudder with disgust when you have seen other people do them."[52]

It is a wonder what Wittgenstein would have made of the martyrs. They were better Wittgensteinians than he. Attalus cried out to the crowds in his death, and the pagans carried the sign.[53]

UNGUARDED TRUTHFULNESS

Once, torture and truth were displayed simultaneously. As Foucault showed, upon the bodies of punished criminals were inscribed not only the truth of the crime committed, but also the judgment of God and the power of the sovereign.[54] Eventu-

49. Ignatius of Antioch *Letter to the Smyrnaeans* 4.

50. Ibid., *Letter to the Ephesians* 18.

51. Monk, *Ludwig Wittgenstein*, 234.

52. Ibid., 580. Cited from *Culture and Value*, 87e.

53. *Martyrs of Lyons* 1.44.

54. Foucault, *Discipline and Punish*, 42–57.

ally, this "penal liturgy" gave way to the display of other truths; in "the multiplicity of scientific discourses, a difficult, infinite relation was then forged that penal justice is still unable to control."[55] Punishment of bodies gave way to care of the soul amid a deluge of specific discourses of expertise. Regarding Christian martyrdom, Foucault's insight is to be accepted with proper nuance. Recalling Augustine and Milbank from the previous chapter: from a theological perspective, what Foucault describes, both before and after penal reform, is the aesthetics of truth. As Milbank says, "knowledge is not a representation of things, but is a relation to events, and an action upon events. Our judgment of the 'truth' of events, according to Augustine in the *Confessions*, is essentially an aesthetic matter."[56] For Milbank, this is undoubtedly on display as ecclesiology, the realistic "metanarrative" beginning with Israel and continuing through Jesus and the church; of which, as members, the martyrs instantiate and exemplify the endurance and (in the church's memory of them) triumph of such a narrative. By this, to use Wells's term, the martyrs are able to overaccept the narratives of their persecutors.

In this section, Milbank and Wells's arguments are rehearsed, yet without Milbank's "meta-"designs. What the martyrs exemplify can certainly be read as ecclesiology as well as overacceptance; however, what is clear is that the martyrs cannot themselves read their actions as ecclesiology or overacceptance. Such a reading is properly the purpose of the church's own subsequent memory of the martyrs. To imagine that the martyrs possessed the rationality of overacceptance while they faced their persecutors would be to misunderstand the precarious truthfulness the martyrs exemplify in the very moment of martyrdom.

55. Ibid., 98.
56. Milbank, *Theology and Social Theory*, 427.

Following Craig Hovey, martyrs display lives lived with a "preference for promise over prediction." That is, martyrs do not willingly suffer and die because of some ideological assumption about the ultimate tide of history that their deaths help instrumentally bring about. Rather, martyrs willingly suffer and die because such living and dying is itself the very mode of their relationship with Jesus. To use the traditional term, martyrdom is the seal of a person's union with Christ, not the catalyst for some larger scheme. The future for martyrs, Hovey suggests, is always surprising "because of the freedom of the promise maker to fulfill the promise, and also the persisting presence of the promise maker to those to whom the promise is made."[57] Such union with the promise maker is itself the *telos* of martyrdom and nothing else. Moreover, this union with Jesus refuses to manipulate history, past or future, as well as the burdens and strictures of the present. As for the persecutors, so too for the martyrs, the future is obscure and the present bewildering:

> When Jesus speaks about the future life of the church, its suffering witness, he is not inviting his disciples to see with a God's-eye view abstracted from their time and place. Instead, he is reorienting the present perception of a people for whom the future arrives in temporal succession in the same way as for anybody else. It is not the esoteric knowledge of the events themselves that constitutes Jesus' special insight or the disciples' privilege. But it is the *meaning* of the events that characterizes the simultaneous invitation and caution extended to the disciples, the places the events find within the larger story in the history of God's salvation. The stress is precisely *not* on the inevitability of the events, but on the surprise given that the ordinary sequence of events is no longer seen to be decisive. Event followed by event, causally connected

57. Hovey, *To Share in the Body*, 140.

by a greater meaning that underwrites the normativity of that meaning—this no longer holds the key to life in the world; it never has.[58]

What the martyrs possess, therefore, is not some secret advance knowledge of the outcome of present circumstances and events, no matter the martyrs' location within an ecclesiology that claims the whole of history. Instead, martyrs possess, within the same time and space as their persecutors, a relationship with Jesus that describes present events in light of a larger promise. The promise by which the martyrs die is not a vindictive hope for some future reckoning; rather, it is only obedience and imitation of Jesus. Perhaps Hovey overstates the nonpredictability of the martyrs' witness in saying, "No knowledge flows from the deaths of martyrs, since martyrdom does not prove anything"[59]; for although the various passions of the martyrs do not instrumentally enact or necessarily even prefigure a future reckoning of the evil of the world, they do at least describe that world as it is, even in the present moment of suffering and death, under the lordship of Jesus Christ. With the rest of creation, the martyrs eagerly groan for the children of God to be revealed,[60] and with Peter the martyrs understand their present sufferings to be the proving of their faith within their hope for Jesus's coming again in glory.[61]

Such groaning and proving, intimated in the New Testament, is just what Chris Huebner describes as the truthful agony of martyrdom that can itself be understood as a "counter-epistemology." Not to be confused with the abrasive necessity of Hegel's metaphysical project, Huebner's suggestion that truth

58. Ibid., 137.

59. Ibid., 147.

60. Rom 8:19.

61. 1 Pet 1:6–7.

names "an essentially agonizing and agonistic reality,"[62] simply illustrates a constant rejection of every totalizing view that may be offered in an attempt to strike some sort of epistemological consensus. What makes for truth, according to Huebner, and what the martyrs exemplify is "dialogical vulnerability."[63] That is, in the martyrs' self-offering, which is both vulnerable and subject not only to the violence of persecutors but also to later praise or condemnation by the church,[64] by that very unguarded performance, martyrdom "constitutes and makes intelligible a certain kind of knowledge." As Huebner insightfully argues, such vulnerability "does away with much of the apparatus of contemporary epistemology—propositional truth claims, justificatory structures, and the like," and unsettles the very suppositions about the sort of subjectivity that supports traditional epistemology.[65] Martyrdom, Huebner argues,

> is not a product or result of what Christians claim to know. Rather, martyrdom names a distinctly Christian way of knowing, a way of knowing that is characteristic of the body of Christ, and in particular, a way of knowing nonviolently, a nonviolent body of knowledge.[66]

According to Huebner, martyrdom's "counter-epistemology" trades "epistemic justification" for the "epistemological virtues of patience and hope."[67] Agreeing with Hovey, in a sense, martyrdom proves nothing, yet it is a proving that is itself a new mode of truthfulness.

62. Huebner, *Precarious Peace*, 134.

63. Ibid., 109.

64. Ibid., 139.

65. Ibid., 137.

66. Ibid., 138.

67. Ibid., 143.

It is here that some descriptive capacity can be attributed to martyrs' speech. Following Hovey and Huebner, martyrdom certainly does not indicate any metaphysical claims of truth; and if martyrdom ever indicates any sort of metanarrative, it does so only in the doxology and memory of the church, and then only precariously. Huebner, perhaps too wary of Milbank's "meta-"designs, rejects narrative schemes as inherently violent,[68] instead referring to the performance of epistemological virtues, which themselves constitute "an agonistic mode of knowledge that proceeds in fragments and ad hoc alliances, not the development of large-scale totalities."[69] Here martyrs' speech as a way of knowing and Wittgenstein's account of language games again coincide. Martyrdom names the fulfillment of a life lived according to the virtues issuing from faith in Jesus and discipleship. Such faith enlivens the complex narrative of Israel and the church, which in turn describes the martyr's present circumstances. Such are the empirical propositions of the martyr's language game, fostering the particular judgments that arise amid various rhetorical and physical conflicts. These judgments vulnerably challenge the dominant language games in which the martyrs find themselves, and even, it may be argued, change them, as in Polycarp's return on the governor's appeal and Attalus's last cry. Yet this changed language game is itself always unguarded, uttered "in the hope of a return that it is powerless of itself to effect."[70] Although the language game has changed in the witness given in martyrdom, suffering and death remain. After being nailed to his cross, the executioner made Pionius an offer, "Change your mind and the nails will be taken out." Giving witness, yet remaining vulnerable, Pionius

68. Ibid., 127.

69. Ibid., 143.

70. Hart, *Beauty of the Infinite*, 443.

answered, "I felt that they are in to stay." Nonetheless, nailed down and dying, Pionius said, "I am hurrying that I may awake all the more quickly, manifesting the resurrection from the dead."[71] The language game had changed, and a dying man talked of resurrection.

PILGRIM HOLINESS

What, then, does this way of knowing look like? How can Attalus's dying judgment that not Christians, but those watching his death were the real cannibals be considered truthful? In this final section it is now possible to trace out a way of living described as pilgrim holiness. The imagery of pilgrimage used here in one sense converges and in another sense diverges from Augustine's classic description of the Church on pilgrimage. For him both the earthly city and the Church "make use of things essential for this mortal life"; however, the Church uses "earthly and temporal things like a pilgrim in a foreign land." Moreover, for Augustine, pilgrim use of earthly peace also "defends and seeks the compromise between human wills in respect of the provisions relevant to the mortal nature of man, so far as may be permitted without detriment to true religion and piety."[72] Here Augustine's notion of pilgrimage diverges from the description offered in this section. Pilgrim use of earthly peace is on dangerous ground when it presumes to understand much less pursue "the provisions relevant to the mortal nature of man" insofar as those provisions are achieved by lights other than discipleship. What is offered here is the description of living virtuously and speaking truthfully and peacefully as a disciple in such a way that renounces the pretension of totalizing violent perspectives,

71. *Martyrdom of Pionius the Presbyter and his Companions* 21.3–4.
72. Augustine *City of God* 19.17.

even renouncing grand or tribal perspectives that need not be total to be violent. Following Huebner, pilgrim holiness is a way of living and knowing according to the epistemological virtues of patience and hope and not after illusory epistemological justifications. Of course, this is an unsettling notion of pilgrimage and of holiness, for it renounces the suggestion that the Church should primarily concern itself with eliminating the fissures, discord, and suffering found in the world. Rather, pilgrim holiness simply and sometimes scandalously (or some would argue irresponsibly) is a way of living according to the virtues of Jesus, leaving compromises and consequences to the merciful God of history. As will be shown below, this makes the Church the community not only of patience, suffering, and hope in daily life; but for the sake of the world, pilgrim holiness makes the Church the community of forgiveness.

Rowan Williams is helpful here. Recalling his time in South Africa, he describes a type of dramatic moral clarity about his position and thinking while living there, of decisively having "to answer certain central questions" regarding Apartheid. Returning to Britain, however, Williams reentered "a context in which it was harder to know what sort of 'resistance' was either possible or constructive." For him it was much more difficult to make moral distinctions and decisions. Coming home, he found himself in a "different moral world under a grey and cloudy sky."[73] Reflecting on this experience, feeling "that we have missed the excitement, that we can never be Christians like *that*,"[74] Williams perceives the danger lurking in the way Christians remember the stories of the martyrs, or even in the way philosophers and theologians recall their systems.

---

73. Williams, *Christ on Trial*, 105.
74. Ibid., 106.

For Williams, martyrdom is not about applying historic and heroic patterns to contemporary situations. Doing this would be trying to seize "possession of our future," installing proud self-imagination victoriously above difficulty and conflict. Martyrdom is not about knowing or even imagining the future.[75] Instead, it is about "freedom from the imperatives of violence."[76] That is, martyrdom names a way of living that exemplifies the belief that Jesus is indeed Lord, and that his lordship frees all life from the economies of sin and domination that constitute the bleak politics of the world. However, this is not a mode of living that follows a grand and sweeping theory of reality. Eschatology focuses upon the return of Jesus in glory before there is ever any speculation of a reckoning of the world's wrongs, and even this speculation is subsumed in the larger story of the unity of God with his people. What this means, for Williams, is that martyrdom "is the ultimate statement of belonging in and to the world as God made it, not to a particular order of earthly authority."[77] Martyrdom is the fulfillment of a life lived particularly according to the judgments arrived at after faith in Jesus. For the person on the path to martyrdom, death is, in a sense, arrived at obliquely. Likewise, descriptions offered by the martyrs are also delivered obliquely, as asides, returns, and quips found in ordinary living. That is, by the lights offered in the narrative of Israel and the Church, encountered in discipleship, daily life becomes a sort of ongoing conversation with the story of salvation. It is the sort of conversation arising from the realization, as Barth said, that Christian existence is "grounded indirectly."[78] Jokes, sayings,

75. Ibid., 114.

76. Ibid., 107.

77. Ibid., 111.

78. Barth, *Church Dogmatics* IV/3.2, 566.

small moral maxims, even wisecracks arising as a result of that embodied sacred narrative's location within an alien story all together comprise a new sort of peaceable knowledge available to the world, revealing that in spite of everything the mercy of the Lord endures forever. Sharing this epistemic disposition with Nietzsche, so Hovey argues, Christian truthfulness, here exemplified in martyrs' speech, "rejects the tendency to find refuge in abstraction, of fleeing from history to the comfortable realm of the transcendent where beliefs fit firmly into tidy systems and so function as their own reward."[79] Instead, Christian truthfulness is aphoristic, or rather confessional and parabolic. Christian truthfulness represents and indicates "knowledge without directly pointing to it, obliquely indicating something beyond the literal words of the story being told." Such is how martyrs' speech operates as an invitation "to the hearer to include herself in its narrative."[80] This is, as David Bentley Hart argues, qualifiedly a postmodern stance, "a rhetoric that is peace, and a truth that is beauty."[81] That is, in the idiom of beauty exemplified in martyrs' speech, most often ordinary and occasionally dramatic, a particularly vulnerable participation in truth is possible. Such is the truthfulness of the martyrs, which as Williams well suggests, emerges from out of artful daily life. Paradoxically, renouncing the principalities of the world in favor of Jesus and discipleship brings a person nearer reality, being finally "most fully at home in creation."[82] Such a person lives out her daily life without need of structural theories, instead living only according to the imitative ways of Jesus and the liturgical rhythms of the church. For the person living according to the

---

79. Hovey, *Nietzsche and Theology*, 33.

80. Ibid., 36.

81. Hart, *Beauty of the Infinite*, 6.

82. Williams, *Christ on Trial*, 107.

judgments leading to martyrdom, her life continues without the "anxiety that if something is *not* done our whole reality will collapse or deliver us into the hands of someone or something else, but out of the inner pressure to 'incarnate' what has been given to us, to give it flesh, voice and locality."[83] The truthfulness of martyrdom is offered close to the particularities, failures, violence, and successes of life. Often pilgrims see things more clearly than natives.

The truthfulness of the martyrs, therefore, issues forth from their patience, from their willingness to wait for their promises, yet with full attention to their world. Such is Warren Smith's reading of Polycarp's martyrdom. In contrast to the zeal of Ignatius and the folly of Quintus, the story of Polycarp's death, according to Smith, exhibits the *ad hoc* and circumstantial quality of martyrdom "according to the gospel." In waiting to be arrested, in the sort of back and forth of flight and return, Polycarp exemplifies discipleship free of strategy and ambition, allowing martyrdom to be the result of "simply faithfulness and hopeful patience in the midst of persecution."[84] Smith insightfully recovers the example of Polycarp's martyrdom as a remedy for reading martyrdom in heroic terms of will to power. Likewise, with Williams, Smith suggests that martyrdom is received only by those who have come close to the art of daily life. "For the saint is content to find God's approval and pleasure in her obedience to those tasks—great or seemingly insignificant—which providence has ordained for her."[85] This by no means calls for quietism,[86] but for lives that obediently and particularly live after the virtues of Jesus and the hopeful

83. Ibid., 110.
84. Smith, "Martyrdom," 185.
85. Ibid., 188.
86. Ibid., 190.

utterances of the church. Following Cyprian, martyrdom is not achieved by human power, but "in the condescension of God." "It is one thing for the spirit to be wanting for martyrdom, and another for martyrdom to have been wanting for the spirit."[87]

Martyrdom, therefore, is the fulfillment of hope and patience received throughout the world in dark streets and ghettos, or in amphitheaters and arenas. Martyrdom today might even be received in hospitals and asylums, or in borderland desert wastes as well as in deadening, banal suburban neighborhoods. As Dorothy Day suggested, martyrdom today is "small, hidden, misunderstood."[88] Wherever martyrdom is received, it is the suggestion of this book that whatever claims Christians have of truthfulness, they are to be discovered in those places where Christians precariously live after the virtues of Jesus without the security of theoretical or political structures. In these places is found the knowledge of a new subjectivity according to the gifts of justification and sanctification, received as a gift in discipleship within the church, and not as subjectivities violently manufactured and even more violently secured by liberal secular politics. And not only is there this knowledge, in martyrdom a piecemeal and occasional knowledge is also received that describes all situations anew as it is ultimately under the reign of God. Such is the truthful speech of Attalus and other martyrs.

Yet there is one final characteristic of this new sort of knowing issuing from the truthfulness of martyrdom. And it is this characteristic that is the very fulfillment of the reconciling mission for glory which Jesus gave to the church, and which finally offers a real and contrasting hope to the many ideological and instrumental portrayals of martyrdom today, and to the violent folly of religious warriors.

87. Cyprian of Carthage *On the Mortality* 17.
88. Dorothy Day, "Inventory," 105.

An interesting feature of the account of the martyrs of Lyons is that when those who had first denied Jesus were placed in prison with those who had made a good confession, those who had failed to confess Jesus were not reviled. Rather, as the account describes it:

> The dead were restored to life through the living; the martyrs brought favour to those who bore no witness, and the virgin Mother experienced much joy in recovering alive those whom she had cast forth stillborn. For through the martyrs those who had denied the faith for the most part went through the same process and were conceived and quickened again in the womb and learned to confess Christ. Alive now and strengthened they came before the tribunal that they might again be questioned by the governor: for God, who does not desire the death of a sinner but shows him the favour of repentance, made it sweet for them.[89]

In the end, because of the truthfulness of the martyrs who believed in the mercy and love of God, even after denials of weakness, Satan was forced to vomit up "all those whom he at first thought he had devoured,"[90] and forgiveness was revealed to be the character of recreated reality. "This is how," notes Augustine, "the citizens of the City of God are restored to health while on pilgrimage on this earth, as they sigh for their Heavenly Country."[91] Thus, the martyrs speak truthfully and in their obedience share in the forgiveness of all violence.

89. *Martyrs of Lyons* 1.45–46.

90. Ibid., 2.6.

91. Augustine *City of God* 15.6.

Re-membering the Church

MARTYRDOM, MEMORY, AND CHRISTIAN UNITY

"They were each given a white robe and told to rest a little
longer, until the number would be complete both of their
fellow servants and of their brothers and sisters . . ."

—Revelation 6:11

REMEMBERING THE MARTYRS

Pothinus, Sanctus, Blandina, Attalus, and others are known
only because someone thought it was important to share their
stories. The account of the martyrs of Lyons, for instance, was
written to Christians in Asia and Phrygia who shared "the same
faith and hope in the redemption."[1] Eusebius introduces this
letter in his *Ecclesiastical History* by contrasting stories of the
martyrs with histories that record only "victories in war and
triumphs over enemies, of the exploits of the commanders and
the heroism of their men." For Eusebius these histories stand
in stark contrast to the stories of the martyrs. Martyrs waged
"peaceful wars," battles fought for the "peace of the soul." In

1. *Martyrs of Lyons* 1.3

contrast to generals, martyrs fought "for truth, rather than for country, for true religion rather than their dear ones." More concerned with invisible battles than visible ones, stories of the early martyrs were inscribed upon "imperishable monuments," somehow preserved by a memory more permanent than the fleeting histories of military victories.[2] Martyr stories were different; they were more than mere history.

Early martyr stories operated within an emerging discourse of Christian personal and cultural identity. These stories were written down and shared. They were woven into the liturgical calendar of the churches and into the homilies of early fathers. The martyrs were exemplary Christians, so their stories were likewise paradigmatic for Christian life. Very few Christians would experience the tortures Blandina faced, but through the prayers of the liturgy or at a martyr's shrine, through moral connections made in a good sermon, or in taking the name of a particular saint, ordinary Christians were formed in the virtues that martyrs exhibited in suffering and death. Martyr stories shaped the imagination of what it meant to be holy. Martyrs performed the Christian story, and by their performance and through the church's memory, they offered an imitable pattern of faithfulness for countless ordinary Christians.

That martyrs were, and remain, powerful examples for Christians is no new thesis. Elizabeth Castelli, for example, explores the collective memory of early Christian martyrdoms as a "form of culture making," in which martyr stories offered slightly variable profiles of Christian identity.[3] Castelli is undoubtedly right that remembering the stories of early Christian martyrs produced a culture in which certain identities flourished and sometimes shifted within the evolving memory of Christians.

2. Eusebius *History of the Church* 5.1.

3. Castelli, *Martyrdom and Memory*, 4.

This book has argued that Christian martyrdom is intelligible first christologically as a hopeful performance of the Christian narrative. Likewise, religious dying either within Islam or Judaism is intelligible only within their particular narrative horizons. To apply only a supposedly neutral sociological description to the martyrdoms of Christians, Muslims, or Jews, inappropriately disregards the very narratives that provided the motives and intelligibility for martyrdom in the first place. Christian martyrdom, for instance, emerges within a particular narrative of Jesus's lordship in which Christian martyrs understood themselves to be faithful. Their task was to live and speak to the ultimate rule of Jesus. This caused conflict with Caesar before whom innumerable martyrs confessed another lord. Further, in this conflict the martyrs' speech exhibited a truthfulness that was experienced as a sort of rhetorical reversal as when Polycarp denounced the atheists, or when Attalus accused the crowd gathered to watch his death of cannibalism. In these verbal exchanges, the narratives martyrs inhabited "overaccepted" the narratives of their persecutors, and in doing this a new and limited language game was disclosed as a testimony to a much larger story of reconciliation than those their persecutors could imagine. Thus, martyrs exemplify both truthfulness and peacefulness in a particularly extraordinary way.

Concluding this extended meditation on the martyrs of Lyons and Vienne, it is appropriate to think about both martyrs and their memory as they relate to the community in which these stories are rendered intelligible—that is, the Church. Certainly, Castelli is right in seeing Christian martyrdom as a powerful formative element within Christian discourse and identity. However, something more theological can be argued here. Emerging repeatedly throughout this book is the Church as the source of intelligibility for martyrdom. Martyrs, in a sense, are the Church's story. Martyrs are not heroes. That is, their lives do not tell their own personal stories; rather, they first tell the story of Israel, Jesus, and the Church. Thus, given that martyrdom is intelligible according to the particular narrative of Israel, Jesus, and the Church; and also given that martyrs' speech in particular discloses that narrative in an exemplary and reconciling fashion, it is possible to suggest that both martyrs' speech and also the Church's memory of martyrs provide not only exemplifications and training in the habits of truthfulness but also in the habits of unity. The martyrs of Lyons left "no pain for their Mother, no strife or conflict for their brothers, but rather joy, peace, harmony, and love." Not only this, the account of these martyrs' testimonies was meant to have the same peaceful influence on those who heard these stories. "Let this be usefully said about the love of these blessed martyrs," the author of the account concludes.[4] The testimony and love of the martyrs had a double effect of peace, and it is this peaceful effect, which provides something for the Church today. Martyrdom and the memory of martyrs do more than create culture and foster subjectivity. Martyrdom and the memory of martyrs help disclose and heal the Church through suffering and forgiveness. Martyrs' speech and martyrs' stories help re-member the Church in a sense. Thus, it is appropriate to argue in conclusion that martyrdom today should be seen in an ecumenical light. That is, if Christian martyrdom is christologically intelligible, then it must also in some sense be ecclesiologically intelligible as well.

RE-MEMBERING THE CHURCH

The ecumenical movement in the twentieth century was a grand and sweeping affair. Filled with heroes, courage, sacrifice,

4. *Martyrs of Lyons* 2.7–8

and moments of historic reconciliation, the ecumenical movement of the last hundred years has done more for the unity of
Christians in a single century than would have been thought
possible after more than a millennium of misunderstanding
and schism. From Edinburgh, Amsterdam, and Uppsala, and
from the 1920 Lambeth Conference to *Unitatis Redintegratio*
of Vatican II, unprecedented steps toward real Christian unity
were taken courageously and sometimes sacrificially. Despite this
remarkable progress, however, the churches have yet to embrace
this movement fully. The ecumenical movement of the previous
century was largely an international movement. Meetings and
conferences were held at a superstructural level; and although
remarkable progress was made doctrinally and also in terms of
simple ecclesiastical courtesy, the fruit of this movement has
largely remained unaccepted in unread documents and brief,
forgotten articles and essays. Today there is neither much talk
of this movement among everyday laity, nor is there very much
energy to learn much about it.

This has caused some to suggest that the age of ecumenism
is over, overwhelmed by a new postmodern globalism that makes
old ecclesial differences seem irrelevant and not even worthy of
the hard and perhaps impossible work of theological reconciliation, which trades in archaic discourses of modernity. This is
certainly correct in a limited sense. For example, although proud
of his work in ecumenical dialogue in the past, Avery Cardinal
Dulles suggests that the old "method of convergence, which
seeks to harmonize the doctrines of each ecclesial tradition on
the basis of shared sources and methods, has nearly exhausted
its potential." For Dulles, "to surmount the remaining barriers
we need a different method, one that invites deeper conversion
on the part of the churches themselves."[5] Talk of conversion,

---

5. Dulles, "Saving Ecumenism from Itself," 26.

of course, echoes John Paul II's encyclical *Ut Unum Sint*. What is needed for ecumenism to proceed in the new century is a willingness to live out the progress of the ecumenical movement on a local level. As Michael Kinnamon and Brian Cope argue, the ecumenism "now emerging will likely be marked not by a single new paradigm but by multiple centres of energy, multiple methodologies, multiple priority concerns." The success of ecumenism in this new century will depend on whether or not varieties of ecumenical efforts will "be effectively taught at the local level of the church."[6] What have been eclipsed, or at least relegated to a minor role, are the superstructural meetings and conferences so very distant from the moral imagination of ordinary people. Ecumenism in this new century will be far less organized, but it will be more organic and surprising. In this new ecumenical era less and less will be done by commissions and conferences while more and more will be achieved by individuals and communities willing to risk Christian unity.

This is precisely where ecumenism and martyrdom come together. Dulles suggests that what is necessary in this new century of ecumenism is a commitment to "testimony," that is, simply to sharing confessions with integrity. According to Dulles, partners in dialogue should not feel compelled to cut any allegedly obstructive elements from their particular theological traditions; rather, participants should feel "free to draw on their own normative sources." Ecumenical partners should simply bear witness to their particular experiences of the gospel. This is an ecumenical vision that trusts less in the coherent convergence of dogmatic traditions achieved in the compromises of conferences and commissions and more in truth and in the Holy Spirit disclosed in witness:

6. Kinnamon and Cope, *Ecumenical Movement*, 8.

> Some will perhaps receive the grace to accept what
> they hear credibly attested as an insight from other
> communities. The witnesses and their hearers need
> not insist on rigorous proof, because very little of our
> faith can be demonstrated by deductive methods.
> Testimony operates by a different logic. We speak of
> what has been graciously manifested to us and what
> we have found to be of value in our relationship with
> God. If others accept what we proclaim, it is because
> our words evoke an echo in them and carry the hall-
> mark of truth.[7]

Dulles here is expressing the ecumenical attitude of the Catholic Church, and it is within Catholic ecumenical documents from Vatican II to the present that the significance of martyrdom for ecumenism is most clearly on display. What is intimated by Dulles and others are new paradigms, less ordered but no less reconciling.

Vatican II was a remarkable council, and in many ways the influence of the council has yet to be felt. For the ecumenical movement, this council marked the Catholic Church's formal entrance into what had been, up to that point, a mostly Protestant movement. Much progress was made between the Catholic Church and the churches of the Reformation as well as with the churches of Eastern Orthodoxy. For this discussion, however, what is most remarkable was what the council understood the nature of Christian unity to be and how it could be achieved. The council asserted that in the Catholic Church the whole church "subsists." Nonetheless, outside the Catholic Church could be found "many elements of sanctification and of truth." These disparate elements of holiness by their very nature belonged to the one Christ and therefore to the one church. Thus, wherever these elements were to be found, they

7. Dulles, "Saving Ecumenism," 27.

were "forces impelling towards Catholic unity."[8] This imperfect unity is grounded in baptism, the council taught, yet among some this unity of Christ has been so intensely experienced in "gifts and graces" of the Holy Spirit that even some non-Catholics have been "strengthened . . . even to the shedding of their blood."[9] For the council, these instances of sanctification and suffering are the seeds of unity. From these witnesses to Christ, both within and without the Catholic Church, come the beauty and attraction of fuller unity. Furthermore, these seeds of unity flourish in the devotion and memory of the Church. "It is not merely by the title of example that we cherish the memory of those in heaven," the council later expressed; "we seek, rather, that by this devotion to the exercise of fraternal charity the union of the whole Church in the Spirit may be strengthened."[10] For the council, both martyrdom and the churches' memory of the martyrs suggest a greater unity than what is experienced in division. For the council, the martyrs are the forerunners and patrons of ecumenism.

John Paul II only further emphasized martyrs' significance for ecumenism in his encyclical *Ut Unum Sint*. Evoking the "courageous witness of so many martyrs of our century," both Catholics and non-Catholics alike, John Paul made clear that these "brothers and sisters of ours, united in the selfless offering of their lives for the Kingdom of God, are the most powerful proof that every factor of division can be transcended and overcome in the total gift of self for the sake of the Gospel."[11] Yet, for the Pope, martyrs both past and present do not merely appeal to some ideological fundamentalism of politically secured

---

8. *Lumen Gentium* § 8. See also *Unitatis Redintegratio* § 4.

9. *Lumen Gentium* § 15. See also *Unitatis Redintegratio* § 4.

10. Ibid., § 50.

11. John Paul II, *Ut Unum Sint* § 1.2.

institutional unity; rather, in the martyrs one sees how unity is received by way of the discovery of truth and the self-offering of love. Love of truth, John Paul emphasizes, "is the deepest dimension of any authentic quest for full communion between Christians."[12] Without truth and love, and without a willingness to suffer for the sake of truth, any appearance of unity is a charade; and this is why the martyrs exemplify unity, for in peaceably suffering for the truth, martyrs bear witness to reconciliation received rather manufactured. Martyrs exhibit what John Paul calls the "dialogue of conversion," living lives "of repentance and absolute trust in the reconciling power of truth, which is Christ." Martyrs "have preserved an attachment to Christ and to the Father so radical and so absolute as to lead even to the shedding of blood."[13] Their witness, John Paul argues, reveals the full communion for which the churches struggle. Their example, active in the memory of the churches, in a sense, re-members the Church:

> In a theocentric vision, we Christians already have a common *martyrology*. This also includes the martyrs of our own century, more numerous than one might think, and it shows how, at a profound level, God preserves communion among the baptized in the supreme demand of faith, manifested in the sacrifice of life itself. The fact that one can die for the faith shows that other demands of the faith can also be met. I have already remarked, and with deep joy, how an imperfect but real communion is preserved and is growing at many levels of ecclesial life. I now add that this communion is already perfect in what we all consider the highest point of the life of grace, *martyria* unto death, the truest communion possible

12. Ibid., § 36.2.
13. Ibid., § 82–83.

with Christ who shed his blood, and by that sacrifice
brings near those who were once far off.[14]

For the Catholic Church, martyrs exhibit truth and the unity of
truth. In those who suffer and die for truth, either as members
of the Catholic Church or not, participation in the unity of
Christ is the result. Their dying is first a witness to the narrative
of Jesus, not to some ideological principle of unity. Protestant
martyrs who died at the hands of Catholics can bear witness to
this singular narrative of Jesus just as well as Catholics who died
at the hands of Protestants. What is necessary is a new collective
memory of the churches, which resists the temptation to rein-
force division but which instead practices forgiveness. Thus, for
ecumenism, martyrs and the churches' memory and devotion
for them play a central role.

THE PEACE OF THE MARTYRS

Like John Paul II before him, Benedict XVI linked martyrdom
with ecumenism. "Thus, in full awareness," he said, "and at
the beginning of his ministry in the church of Rome that Peter
bathed in his blood, the current successor assumed as his pri-
mary commitment that of working tirelessly toward the recon-
stitution of the full and visible unity of all Christ's followers."
Further, Benedict repeated his successor's call for the "purification of memory."[15] Desire for the truth and unity for which
Christ prayed, even to the point of death, and the church's
practice of memory: these, in Benedict's mind, are the necessary
conditions for truth and unity in a reconciled church.

The martyrs put these virtues on display, and the church
remembers them. The martyrs live as if truth and justice, trans-

14. Ibid., § 84.
15. Thornton and Varenne, *Essential Pope Benedict XVI*, 28.

figured in light of the confession that Jesus is Lord, are more significant than their lives, and the church is encouraged to live truthfully.[16] The martyrs more fully live out the narrative of Jesus and the church. They exemplify the ultimate narrative of Christ. The purpose of this book has been to show this and to show how this simple performance of narrative, or rather, this simple performance of hope, makes for the reconciling re-description of reality. "Peace they had always loved, and it was peace which they commended to us for ever."[17] This is the real import of martyrdom. This is why the martyrs forgave those around them. Martyrs do not die for disembodied principles. Martyrs die because they live as if Jesus is truly Lord and as if the Church is truly one. Martyrs forgive their persecutors and even those who have fallen because Jesus and the Church are more real and lasting than even violence and failure. This is the peace the martyrs share, the peace of the Church.

Of course, to connect martyrs with peace is a hard sell now-adays. That anything but purely inward religion begets violence is almost universally accepted, even by many people of faith. Martyrdom, by and large, connotes tragic and dangerous abso-lutism, something to be discouraged among citizens of liberal democracies. To suggest that martyrs and remembering martyrs cultivates peace is absurd to many.

In a certain sense this is right. Martyrdom is certainly at odds with much of the violent pragmatism of liberal politics. In the first chapter of this book, it was argued that martyrs could not be policed by the narratives of liberal politics. Likewise, in turn, it would be inappropriate to seek a hallowed or respected place for martyrdom within an alien philosophical and political discourse. To hold martyrs up as exemplary or even as accept-able for liberal politics would be to desire the same sociological

16. Benedict XVI, *Spe Salvi* § 38–39.

17. *The Martyrs of Lyons* 2.7.

incoherence so adamantly rejected. It is true: martyrs often make bad citizens.

However, they do make good saints. And this is the reason for concluding a book on martyrdom by talking about ecumenism. Given that martyrs live out the story of Christ, and given that they speak in their limited ways by the lights of their particular narrative, perhaps it is worthwhile to remember that it is first to the Church that the martyrs relate and not to some vague, sociologically described humanism. To the crowds, Blandina appeared to be a remarkably strong woman at best,[18] while Pothinus was largely perceived to be a foolish old man. The author of the story does not spend very much time describing the crowds other than to report either their amazement or rabid cruelty. Their reactions did not seem to matter very much. What mattered was that Blandina's fellow Christians saw Christ in her as she hung on a post in the form of a cross.[19] What mattered more than the violence of the crowed was that Pothinus received their abuse "as though he were Christ himself." Indeed, it did not seem to concern Pothinus very much at all whether or not his death made sense. All he answered the governor when asked about the "Christian god" he was suffering for was "If you are worthy, you will know."[20] It was not important that anyone made sense of these martyrs. What mattered was their identity with Christ in obedience, suffering, and death, and that the Church remembered them. This was all that was needed.

Christian martyrdom should be renewed in the church's memory and in the imagination of individual Christians. Martyrs should not be relegated to an embarrassing and unenlightened past, nor should they be made to fit sociologically

18. Ibid., 1.56.
19. Ibid., 1.41.
20. Ibid., 1.30–31.

and politically acceptable models. Rather, martyrs should be re-membered for their witness to Jesus. They should be celebrated for their hope in the narrative of the Church. Martyrs should be embraced as those who disclose and also compel the unity of all Christians, of all those who inhabit the same narrative horizon. This is the first gift of the martyrs—unity in Christ. Only when the Church receives this gift, when Christians are willing to inhabit the narrative of the Church in the face of every other di-visive narrative of nation, race, class, denomination, or gender, will they be able to give witness to what is believed to be a more lasting peace, which passes all understanding.

Bibliography

Abdel Haleem, M. A. S., translator. *The Qur'an*. Oxford: Oxford University Press, 2004.

The Acts of the Scillitan Martyrs. In *Acts of the Christian Martyrs*, edited and translated by Herbert Musurillo, 86–89. Oxford Early Christian Texts. Oxford: Oxford University Press, 1972.

Ambrose. *Death as a Good*. Translated by Michael P. McHugh. *Seven Exegetical Works*. The Fathers of the Church Series 65. Washington, DC: Catholic University of America Press, 1972.

Arendt, Hannah. *The Origins of Totalitarianism*. New York: Harcourt, 1976.

Asad, Talal. *Formations of the Secular: Christianity, Islam, Modernity*. Cultural Memory in the Present. Stanford: Stanford University Press, 2003.

———. *On Suicide Bombing*. Wellek Library Series. New York: Columbia University Press, 2007.

Augustine. *City of God*. Translated by Henry Bettenson. London: Penguin, 1984.

———. *Teaching Christianity (De Doctrina Christiana)*. The Works of Saint Augustine I/11. Translated by Edmund Hill. Hyde Park, NY: New City, 1996.

———. *The Trinity (De Trinitate)*. Translated by Edmund Hill. The Works of Saint Augustine I/5. Hyde Park, NY: New City, 1991.

Barth, Karl. *Church Dogmatics* IV/3.2. Translated by G. W. Bromiley. Edinburgh: T. & T. Clark, 1997.

Bauman, Zygmunt. *Liquid Modernity*. Cambridge: Polity, 2000.

Benedict XVI. *Spe Salvi*. Boston: Pauline, 2007.

Berthold, G. C. "Did Maximus the Confessor Know Augustine?" In *Studia Patristica* 17.1, edited by Elizabeth Livingstone, 14–17. Oxford: Pergamon, 1982.

Blackburn, Simon. *Truth: A Guide*. Oxford: Oxford University Press, 2005.

Bowersock, G. W. *Martyrdom and Rome*. Wiles Lectures. Cambridge: Cambridge University Press, 1995.

Boyarin, Daniel. *Dying for God: Martyrdom and the Making of Christianity*. Figurae. Stanford: Stanford University Press, 1999.

Brown, Daniel. "Martyrdom in Sunni Revivalist Thought." In *Sacrificing the Self: Perspectives on Martyrdom and Religion*, edited by Margaret Cormack, 107–17. Oxford: Oxford University Press, 2002.

Burbidge, John. W. *Hegel's Systematic Contingency*. New York: Palgrave Macmillan, 2007.

Castelli, Elizabeth. *Martyrdom and Memory: Early Christian Culture Making*. Gender, Theory, and Religion. New York: Columbia University Press, 2004.

Clement of Alexandria. *The Stromata*. Edited by Alexander Roberts and James Donaldson, Ante-Nicene Fathers 2:409–43. Edinburgh: T. & T. Clark, 1979.

Cook, David. "The Implications of 'Martyrdom Operations' for Contemporary Islam." *Journal of Religious Ethics* 32 (2004) 129–51.

———. *Martyrdom in Islam*. Themes in Islamic History. Cambridge: Cambridge University Press, 2007.

Cyprian of Carthage. *On the Mortality*. Translated by Ernest Wallis. Ante-Nicene Fathers 5:469–75. Edinburgh: T. & T. Clark, 1979.

Dawkins, Richard. *The God Delusion*. Boston: Houghton Mifflin, 2006.

Day, Dorothy. "Inventory." In *By Little and By Little: The Selected Writings of Dorothy Day*, edited by Robert Ellsberg, 104–5. New York: Knopf, 1983.

Dennett, Daniel. *Breaking the Spell: Religion as a Natural Phenomenon*. New York: Viking, 2006.

Dulles, Avery Cardinal. "Saving Ecumenism from Itself." *First Things* 178 (2007) 23–27.

Eusebius. *The History of the Church*. Translated by G. A. Williamson and Andrew Louth. London: Penguin, 1989.

Foucault, Michel. *Discipline and Punish: The Birth of the Prison*. New York: Vintage, 1995.

Fox, Michael Allen. *The Accessible Hegel*. New York: Humanity, 2005.

Frend, W. H. C. *Martyrdom and Persecution in the Early Church: A Study of a Conflict from the Maccabees to Donatus*. Oxford: Blackwell, 1965.

Goldziher, Ignaz. *Muslim Studies*. 2 vols. Translated by C. R. Barber and S. M. Stern. Edited by S. M. Stern. London: Allen & Unwin, 1968–71.

Harris, Sam. *The End of Faith: Religion, Terror, and the Future of Reason.* New York: Norton, 2005.

Hart, David Bentley. *The Beauty of the Infinite: The Aesthetics of Christian Truth.* Grand Rapids: Eerdmans, 2003.

Hartshorne, M. Holmes. *Kierkegaard, Godly Deceiver: The Nature and Meaning of His Pseudonymous Writings.* New York: Columbia University Press, 1990.

Hauerwas, Stanley, and Charles Pinches. *Christians among the Virtues: Theological Conversations with Ancient and Modern Ethics.* Notre Dame: Notre Dame University Press, 1997.

Hauerwas, Stanley, and Samuel Wells. "Christian Ethics as Informed Prayer." In *The Blackwell Companion to Christian Ethics*, edited by Stanley Hauerwas and Samuel Wells, 3–12. Oxford: Blackwell, 2006.

Hegel, G. W. F. *Phenomenology of Spirit.* Translated by A. V. Miller. Oxford: Oxford University Press, 1977.

———. *Philosophy of History.* Translated by J. Sibree. New York: Dover, 1956.

Hitchens, Christopher. *God is Not Great: How Religion Poisons Everything.* New York: Twelve, 2007.

Hovey, Craig. *Nietzsche and Theology.* Philosophy and Theology. New York: T. & T. Clark, 2008.

———. *To Share in the Body: A Theology of Martyrdom for Today's Church.* Grand Rapids: Brazos, 2008.

Huebner, Chris K. *A Precarious Peace: Yoderian Explorations on Theology, Knowledge, and Identity.* Polyglossia. Scottdale, PA: Herald, 2006.

Ignatius of Antioch. *Letter to the Ephesians.* In *Early Christian Writings: The Apostolic Fathers*, translated by Maxwell Stanforth and Andrew Louth, 59–68. London: Penguin, 1987.

———. *Letter to the Romans.* In *Early Christian Writings: The Apostolic Fathers*, translated by Maxwell Stanforth and Andrew Louth, 83–89. London: Penguin, 1987.

———. *Letter to the Smyrnaeans.* In *Early Christian Writings: The Apostolic Fathers*, translated by Maxwell Stanforth and Andrew Louth, 99–105. London: Penguin, 1987.

———. *Letter to the Trallians.* In *Early Christian Writings: The Apostolic Fathers*, translated by Maxwell Stanforth and Andrew Louth, 77–82. London: Penguin, 1987.

John Paul II. *Ut Unum Sint*. In *The Encyclicals of John Paul II*, edited by J. Michael Miller, 914–76. Huntington, IN: Our Sunday Visitor, 1996.

Kierkegaard, Søren. *Concluding Unscientific Postscript to Philosophical Fragments*. Translated by Howard V. Hong and Edna H. Hong. Kierkegaard's Writings 12. Princeton: Princeton University Press, 1992.

Kinnamon, Michael, and Brian E. Cope. *The Ecumenical Movement*. Grand Rapids: Eerdmans, 1997.

Khosrokhavar, Farhad. *Suicide Bombers: Allah's New Martyrs*. Translated by David Macey. London: Pluto, 2005.

Lazenby, J. Mark. *The Early Wittgenstein on Religion*. London: Continuum, 2006.

Lewinstein, Keith. "The Revaluation of Martyrdom in Early Islam." In *Sacrificing the Self: Perspectives on Martyrdom and Religion*, edited by Margaret Cormack, 78–91. Oxford: Oxford University Press, 2002.

Lewis, Bernard. *The Middle East: A Brief History of the Last 2,000 Years*. New York: Scribner, 2003.

Lumen Gentium. In *Vatican Council II: The Conciliar and Post Conciliar Documents*, edited by Austin Flannery, 350–423. Grand Rapids: Eerdmans, 1992.

MacIntyre, Alasdair. *Three Rival Versions of Moral Enquiry: Encyclopedia, Genealogy and Tradition*. Notre Dame: Notre Dame University Press, 1990.

Malone, Edward. *The Monk and the Martyr: The Monk as the Successor of the Martyr*. Washington, DC: Catholic University of America Press, 1950.

The Martyrdom of Pionius the Presbyter and His Companions. In *Acts of the Christian Martyrs*, edited and translated by Herbert Musurillo, 136–67. Oxford Early Christian Texts. Oxford: Oxford University Press, 1972.

The Martyrdom of Saints Perpetua and Felicitas. In *Acts of the Christian Martyrs*, edited and translated by Herbert Musurillo, 106–31. Oxford Early Christian Texts. Oxford: Oxford University Press, 1972.

The Martyrdom of St. Polycarp. In *Acts of the Christian Martyrs*, edited and translated by Herbert Musurillo, 2–21. Oxford Early Christian Texts. Oxford: Oxford University Press, 1972.

The Martyrs of Lyons. In *Acts of the Christian Martyrs*, edited and translated by Herbert Musurillo, 62–85. Oxford Early Christian Texts. Oxford: Oxford University Press, 1972.

Maximus the Confessor. *On the Cosmic Mystery of Jesus Christ: Selected Writings from St. Maximus the Confessor*. Translated by Paul Blowers and Robert Wilken. Crestwood, NY: St. Vladimir's Seminary Press, 2003.

Milbank, John. *Theology and Social Theory: Beyond Secular Reason*. Signposts in Theology. Oxford: Blackwell, 1990.

Monk, Ray. *Ludwig Wittgenstein: The Duty of Genius*. New York: Penguin, 1990.

Nietzsche, Friedrich. *The Antichrist: An Essay Towards a Criticism of Christianity*. Translated by Thomas Common. New York: Dover, 2004.

————. *On the Genealogy of Morals*. Translated by Walter Kaufmann and R. J. Hollingdale. New York: Vintage, 1967.

Origen. *Against Celsus*. Translated by Frederick Crombie. Ante-Nicene Fathers 4:395–670. Edinburgh: T. & T. Clark, 1979.

Perkins, Judith. *The Suffering Self: Pain and Narrative in the Early Christian Era*. London: Routledge, 1995.

Plato. *Complete Works*. Edited by John M. Cooper. Indianapolis: Hackett, 1997.

Popper, Karl R. *The Open Society and Its Enemies*. 2 vols. Princeton: Princeton University Press, 1971.

Rhee, Helen. *Early Christian Literature: Christ and Culture in the Second and Third Centuries*. London: Routledge, 2005.

Scott, James C. *Domination and the Arts of Resistance: Hidden Transcripts*. New Haven: Yale University Press, 1990.

Smith, J. Warren. "Martyrdom: Self-Denial or Self-Exaltation? Motives for Self-Sacrifice from Homer to Polycarp a Theological Reflection." *Modern Theology* 22 (2006) 169–96.

Tertullian. *Ad Martyras*. Edited by Allan Menzies. Ante-Nicene Fathers 3:693–96. Edinburgh: T. & T. Clark, 1979.

————. *To Scapula*. Edited by Allan Menzies. Ante-Nicene Fathers 3:105–8. Edinburgh: T. & T. Clark, 1979.

Thornton, John F., and Susan B. Varenne, editors. *The Essential Pope Benedict XVI: His Central Writings and Speeches*. New York: HarperOne, 2007.

Unitatis Redintegratio. In *Vatican Council II: The Conciliar and Post Conciliar Documents*, edited by Austin Flannery, 452–70. Grand Rapids: Eerdmans, 1992.

Weiner, Eugene, and Anita Weiner. *The Martyr's Conviction: A Sociological Analysis*. Atlanta: Scholars, 1990.

Wells, Samuel. "The Disarming Virtue of Stanley Hauerwas." *Scottish Journal of Theology* 52 (1999) 82–88.

————. *Improvisation: The Drama of Christian Ethics*. Grand Rapids: Brazos, 2004.

Wensinck, A. J. *The Oriental Doctrine of the Martyrs*. Mededeelingen der Koninklijke Akademie van Wetenschappen, Afdeeling Letterkunde 53:6. Amsterdam, 1921.

West, David. *An Introduction to Continental Philosophy*. Cambridge: Polity, 1996.

Williams, Rowan. *Christ on Trial: How the Gospel Unsettles Our Judgment*. Grand Rapids: Eerdmans, 2000.

Wittgenstein, Ludwig. *Culture and Value*. Translated by Peter Winch. Chicago: University of Chicago Press, 1984.

———. *On Certainty*. Translated by Denis Paul and G. E. M. Anscombe. New York: Harper & Row, 1972.

———. *Wittgenstein's Tractatus*. Translated by Daniel Kolak. London: Mayfield, 1998.

Yoder, John Howard. *Body Politics: Five Practices of the Christian Community before the Watching World*. Scottdale, PA: Herald, 1992.

———. "How H. Richard Niebuhr Reasoned: A Critique of *Christ and Culture*." In *Authentic Transformation: A New Vision of Christ and Culture*, edited by Glen H. Stassen, D. M. Yeager, and John Howard Yoder, 31–89. Nashville: Abingdon, 1996.

———. *The Original Revolution: Essays on Christian Pacifism*. Scottdale, PA: Herald, 2003.

Young, Robin Darling. *In Procession before the World: Martyrdom as Public Liturgy in Early Christianity*. Milwaukee: Marquette University Press, 2001.